T0339706

SMOKESCREEN

SMOKESCREEN

THE US, NATO AND
THE ILLEGITIMATE USE OF FORCE

PAUL F.J. ARANAS

Algora Publishing
New York

Library of Congress Cataloging-in-Publication Data —

Aranas, Paul F. J.
    Smokescreen: The U.S., NATO and the illegitimate use of force / Paul F.J.
Aranas.
        p. cm.
    Includes bibliographical references and index.
    ISBN 978-0-87586-895-0 (hard cover: alk. paper)—ISBN 978-0-87586-
894-3 (soft cover: alk. paper)—ISBN 978-0-87586-896-7 (ebook) 1. Intervention
(International law) 2. Humanitarian intervention. 3. Peacekeeping forces. 4.
Preemptive attack (Military science) 5. United States—Military policy. 6.
North Atlantic Treaty Organization—Military policy. I. Title.
    JZ6368.A73 2012
    327.1'60973—dc23
                                2012001780

For my parents

TABLE OF CONTENTS

INTRODUCTION

Foreign military interventions waged with purported altruistic aims have antithetically resulted, almost without exception, in
acute humanitarian crises with death, destruction, and suffering far
surpassing the status quo ante. The 2003 U.S. and British invasion
and occupation of Iraq resulted in the deaths of over a million Iraqi
civilians and created millions of refugees, while the George W. Bush
administration claimed, at least in part, to be acting on behalf of the
Iraqi population to help free them from their government. Since the
Industrial Revolution, powerful states have almost without exception provided justifications for imposition and conquest. European
colonialists explained their policy as a "civilizing mission" bringing proper behavior and culture to "savages" (Kohn 2008). Murphy
(1990, p. 536) writes that during World War II "...German expansion was at least in the earliest stages of the war, rhetorically rooted
in a historical-cum-ethnic claim." From his initial ethnic claims,
Hitler would expand his justifications for territorial expansion to
include, first, saving Europe from Bolshevism and, next, spreading
Christian values eastward as the "savior of Christianity and the
Church" (Domarus 1997, p. 1957).

The nature of these criminal conquests had nothing to do with "civilizing" populations or spreading Christian values and saving Christianity, but was rooted in economic and geo-strategic gain. Since the Industrial Revolution, few, if any, exceptions exist of states refusing to employ altruistic rationales to justify predatory conquest. The Belgians in the Congo may be one exception as their main justification for colonial domination was that it would bring "profit for the metropolis" (Gondola 2002, p. 78). But even the Belgians justified their brutal policy by claiming "Europeans had a *mission civilisatrice* (civilizing mission) based on Christianization and education to perform in Africa" (Gondola 2002, p. 78).

Justifications and some standards have changed: in the twenty first century, regardless of any rhetoric, the consensus is that the international community would not tolerate slavery, explicit colonialism, or a state unambiguously spreading religion through the use of force. Governments employ new justifications to create a perception of legitimacy for actions that violate accepted norms.

Numerous states have transgressed the rules and norms codified in the U.N. Charter; however, the most flagrant violators, to varying degrees, include governments entrusted with the primary responsibility for the maintenance of peace, permanent members of the U.N. Security Council. The most routine transgressor of international law, the United States, ironically boasts to act as world defender of human rights and democracy. In 2007, an international poll conducted by the Pew Research Center found that "distrust of the United States had intensified across the world" (Bortin 2007, p. A12). Respondents to the poll, which surpassed more than 45,000 people, stated their desire for the United States to withdraw its military from Iraq and a termination to U.S. and NATO intervention in Afghanistan.

The George W. Bush administration highlighted these transgressions, with his administration's antipathy to multilateralism and his undiplomatic rhetoric. This resulted in two things: it brought attention to unchanging American imperial policy, that had been better masked by the Clinton administration, and it reminded Washington's traditional European allies of two uncomfortable truths: Washington views European governments as subservient and rhetoric concerning global human rights and democracy is a tool for American business interests. The G.W. Bush administration brazenly refused to participate in agenda items that are widely viewed as positive for the global community. In Bush's first six months in office, he opted not to join the Kyoto Protocol on climate change, threatened to revoke the 1972 Anti-Ballistic Missile Treaty, and repealed the signature of the United States for the creation of the International Criminal Court. After September 11, the United States, in violation of some of the most important international treaties, kept prisoners for indefinite sentences in Guantanamo Bay without trial or due process, unilaterally invaded Iraq, brutally abused prisoners at Abu Ghraib prison in Iraq, operated secret CIA prisons in Europe, and rendered prisoners for torture, among other violations of international law. Yale Law Professor Oona A. Hathaway argues that in these violations of international law "lies a comprehensive vision of international law, one that treats international law not as a means of achieving American objectives but as an unnecessary and unjustified limitation on the exercise of American power" (Hathaway 2007, p. 35-36). The 2005 Pentagon National Defense Strategy states, "Our strength as a nation state will continue to be challenged by those who employ a strategy of the weak using international fora, judicial processes, and terrorism" (Hathaway 2007, p. 36). In this view, international law, rules, and regulations are seen as a threat to U.S. national interests. Although the Bush administration reached new heights with its disregard for multilateralism among allies, gross violations of international norms and the principle of universality are certainly not isolated to the Republican Party. Democratic administrations have consistently violated fundamental norms of international relations. President Barack Obama expanded on many of George W. Bush's most blatant violations of international law: drone attacks on Pakistan, Yemen, and Somalia; torture in Bagram Prison in Afghanistan; indefinite detention; targeted assassinations; and extraordinary rendition.

Power and Legitimacy

A power relationship that lacks legitimacy will eventually collapse, because those required to support that particular system of power will, at some point, cease to cooperate. The eighteenth-century philosopher Rousseau explained right versus might in his classic work *The Social Contract*:

> Let us suppose for a moment that this alleged right is valid. I say that the result would be completely senseless. For as soon as right is founded on force, the effect will alter with its cause; any force that is stronger than the first must have right on its side in its turn. As soon as anyone is able to disobey with impunity he may do so legitimately, and since the strongest is always right the only question is how to ensure that one is the strongest. But what kind of right is it that is extinguished when that strength is lost? If we must obey because of force we have no need to obey out of duty, and if we are no longer forced to obey then we no longer have any obligation to do so. It can be seen therefore that the word "right" adds nothing to force; it has no meaning at all here (Rousseau, 1998, p. 8).

Traditionally, Weber has been the starting point for discussing legitimacy within the field of political science and political sociology. Inquiry into the nature of legitimacy may often be limited to Weber's definition alone, which relegates the definition of *legitimacy* to the perception of legitimacy. Weber (1956, pp. 23, 157, 659; 1958, p. 193) defines legitimacy as "legitimitätsglaube" (a belief in legitimacy); he defines legitimate power as power "als legitim angesehen" (that is regarded as legitimate). Social scientists adopt Weber's definition because they are wary of universal truths and are trained to separate their beliefs and values systems from the cases they study, and they examine legitimacy within the context of particular societies throughout history. Moral and political philosophers, on the other hand, are concerned with legitimacy within a universal context. Beetham (1991, pp. 8-11) argues that Weber's influence on the subject of legitimacy "has been an almost unqualified disaster," and that the confusion of the nature of legitimacy stems from Weber's definition, which is shortsighted due to lack of any consideration for aspects pertaining to legitimacy that are completely separate from belief.

Beetham (1991, p. 11) opposes Weber's definition, "the perception of legitimacy" on the grounds that "a given power relationship is not legitimate because people believe in its legitimacy, but because it can be justified in terms of their beliefs." Weber ignores components that are not associated with belief, such as legal validity and consent. Legal validity exists when power is obtained or employed within the constraints of the law. Consent is demonstrated by subordinate actors willfully acknowledging the legitimacy of the power in question through observable actions, such as voting in elections, public agreement, making oaths of allegiances, and other such behavior. These combined elements result in legal validity, or rules justified by shared beliefs of both dominant and subordinate, with evidence of consent from the subordinate (Beetham (1991, p 11-16). Beetham argues that it is these three elements that make an entity legitimate:

> For power to be fully legitimate, then three conditions are required: its conformity to established rules; the justifiability of the reference to shared beliefs; the express consent of the subordinate, or of the most significant among them, to the particular relations of power. All three components contribute to legitimacy, though the extent to which they are realized in a given context will be a matter of degree. Legitimacy is not an all or nothing affair (Beetham 1991, p. 19-20).

Weber's definition empties the concept of its moral content or objective reference. To define the concept of legitimacy as 'a belief in legitimacy' reduces it to a public relations campaign on behalf of the most powerful. Beetham has provided a more accurate and objective definition of legitimacy. Unfortunately, in actual practice, legitimacy is reduced to the perception of legitimacy, which may, at times, actually be a false legitimacy masquerading as a legitimate course of action.

The Media and the Perception of Legitimacy

During the 1983 U.S. invasion of Grenada, the Pentagon barred journalists from Grenada until the third day of the operation and only allowed a media pool of fifteen journalists access to the island. They were confined to the Point Salines airport (Crandall 2006, p. 158). The media fed the American public Pentagon approved images and stories: children celebrating, weapons stockpiles, and Cuban prisoners.

The media and the military developed a tense relationship during the Grenada operation. The military, while publicly stating that the media restriction was for the safety of reporters, felt that the press was intent on damaging the image of the operation. Media outlets became suspicious and concerned that the military was concealing information, while the Pentagon publicly argued that the restrictions were for the safety of journalists. Members of the press corps did not take that explanation seriously as American journalists had braved dangerous conflict zones before, including the landing in Normandy during World War II and the battlefields of Vietnam. But it was just those horrific scenes the Pentagon wanted to avoid — the stories that had damaged the image of the U.S. military during the Vietnam War. Therefore, the Pentagon, learning from British press restrictions during the Falklands War, decided to prohibit any coverage that could be interpreted as critical of the operation. The U.S. military controlled what access reporters had on the island.

Ultimately, the Reagan administration permitted the media access to Grenada because of "intense pressure" from Congress; however, the permission came a week after the invasion began (Crandall 2006, p. 159). The *New York Times* labeled the operation in Grenada the "off the record war," and the *Washington Post* wrote the operation was a "secret war, like a secret government is antithetical to [an] open society. It is absolutely outrageous" (Crandall 2006, p. 159). The restriction during the invasion of Grenada would serve as a starting point and model for serious curtailments of press freedom during U.S. military operations. Richard Reeves, one of the only syndicated columnists to adamantly oppose the invasion of Grenada, said that it was in Grenada that "the modern U.S. military was first able to use force — pointing its guns at American reporters and cameras — to totally control what Americans knew about a military action" (Johns and Johnson 1994, p. 65). Reeves described scenes of reporters attempting to make their way to Grenada by boat only to be stopped by the U.S. military and threatened to be "blown out of the water" if they continued toward the island (Johns and Johnson 1994, p. 65).

During the 1989 U.S. invasion of Panama, the "compromise" between the outright censorship during the Grenada operation and a "free press" became the creation of a "media pool." The media pool system put the control completely in the hands of the U.S. military while still appearing to adhere to the democratic ideals of a free press. In the media pool system, the military decided who could be in the pool, the rules of their participation, where they went, and when they would be "activated" and "deactivated" (Johns & Johnson 1994, p. 65). The Reagan administration had set down some rules for using media pools during conflict, but those rules were disregarded during the invasion of Panama. In Panama, Southern Command was responsible for the media pool, which had no civilian accompaniment, violating a rule promulgated by the Reagan administration. Southern Command became bothered by what they felt were annoying journalists interfering in their military operation. The pool of seven journalists arrived four hours after the launch of the invasion. They were kept in a windowless room for several hours and were not permitted to file a dispatch for six hours after being detained (Johns & Johnson 1994, p. 65). The journalists said that during the first day of the invasion they were escorted to places where the action had ceased and only witnessed fighting when the driver happened to lose his way (Johns & Johnson 1994, p. 65).

Once censored by government, news outlets have become, above all, business enterprises that prioritize ad revenue and ratings above objective content, thus becoming their own censors. Additionally, media executives and board members of media-related conglomerates maintain close connections with the U.S. foreign policy establishment and the military industry. Some media-owning corporations are themselves weapons manufacturers. For example, in fiscal year 2003, during the U.S. British invasion of Iraq, the Pentagon ranked General Electric (GE), then-majority owner of the National

Broadcasting Company (NBC), eighth in military contracts at $2.8 billion (Solomon 2005, p. 114). The mainstream media, far from being a dependable source to investigate governmental deception or to report international affairs as objectively as possible, relies heavily on official sources and often operates as a de facto public relations machine for Washington, especially in times of war.

United Nations Legitimacy

Power has shaped legitimacy based on Weber's definition, a false legitimacy, which has shunned objective criteria, and resulted in massive death and destruction through wars waged with justifications propagated by the offending states and these justifications have been magnified by the mass media, which has effectively become a public relations apparatus of government. This need not be the case as the world is fortunate to have objective criteria in the form of United Nations law, albeit without any overarching enforcement mechanism. However, the root of the problem does not lie in the lack of enforcement but in the mentality that views legitimacy within a Weberian framework. If legitimacy, based on objective criteria in this book, was promoted in the educational system and media, enforcement would follow as a result of internal and external pressure on governments to be responsible international actors.

The United Nations Charter is "a treaty under international law" (Simma 1994, p. 261). The U.N. is separate from all other international institutions because of its international legal personality attributed by the International Court of Justice (ICJ). The ICJ states that the U.N. possesses "a large measure of international personality and the capacity to operate upon an international plane" (Simma 1994, p. 27). The Vienna Convention on the Law of the Treaties (VCLT) also applies to the United Nations Charter both for states that have ratified the VCLT and for those that have not via international customary law. This book aims to demonstrate the difference between that objective reference and the false perception of legitimacy that has created a thick smokescreen in front of the international community.

CHAPTER ONE: THE FOUNDATION

In February 1945, the Big Three-- Russia, Britain, and the United States-- met in the Crimea to negotiate issues relating to the war, the post-war plans for Germany, and the creation of the new world organization. During the discussion on General Assembly (GA) seats, the Soviet delegation embarrassed the British representatives by inquiring about Britain's colonial dominions — especially India. Churchill was adamant that India obtain a seat in the General Assembly but rejected any notion of Indian independence. Roosevelt understood that the British could not object to the proposal while maintaining a colonial empire, and despite opposing the first Russian proposal at Dumbarton, they would accept Moscow's request of two or three extra seats. Churchill accepted the Soviet proposal at once, uneasy about Britain's many dominions (Schlesinger 2003, p. 59).

Stalin said he would never assent to small countries dictating judgments to the Great Powers, and while he believed small countries were worthy of having their rights protected, the Great Powers had the epic responsibility of maintaining world peace. Churchill and Roosevelt agreed, but Churchill added, "The eagle should permit the small birds to sing, and care not wherefor they sang" (Stettinius 1949, p. 112). Stalin responded, "Yugoslavia, Albania, and such small countries do not deserve to be at this table. . . .Do you want Albania to have the same status as the United States? What has Albania done in this war to merit such a standing? We three have to decide how to keep the peace of the world, and it will not be kept unless we three decide to do it" (Stettinius 1949, p. 112). Stalin inquired what the British government's reaction would be if China raised the issue of the return of Hong Kong or if Egypt requested the United Kingdom to return the Suez Canal, and he stated that Churchill was mistaken if he imagined Egypt and China being satisfied by just expressing opinions. They would want a favorable vote, Stalin declared. Churchill said that the United States, the Soviet Union, and the United Kingdom were great powers and were protected by the veto, and they should allow the other nations the right to state their opinions (Beitzell 1970, pp. 78-80). Stalin cautioned the Prime Minister that Egypt and China would have supporters in the Assembly. The Russians were aware that everything would be done in the new organization by a vote, and ascribed great value to the discussions on voting procedure. The Prime Minister and U.S. Secretary of State Edward Stettinius assured Stalin that the United Nations would never be turned against any of the permanent members.

The American delegation raised the concept of trusteeships to the British and Churchill exploded and exclaimed that the United Kingdom dismissed any notions of trusteeships relating to the British Empire. Churchill defended the British Empire throughout the meetings. Roosevelt urged the British to give up Hong Kong "as a measure of goodwill", but British Foreign Secretary Eden countered and charged that President Roosevelt had not offered any "reciprocal gestures" (Clemens 1970, p. 218).

Churchill became livid when Stettinius noted that an agreement had been reached among P-5 Foreign Ministers to hold consultations, prior to the San Francisco Conference, on the process and machinery of trusteeships and dependant areas. He disagreed with everything Stettinius had in his brief on trusteeships. Roosevelt told Churchill that he had not even given Stettinius a chance to complete his sentence. Stettinius (1949, p. 236) reported that Churchill carried on with his objection, saying that he had been unaware of these ideas up until then and that "under no circumstances would he ever consent to the fumbling fingers of forty or fifty nations prying into the life's existence of the British Empire. As long as he was Prime Minister, he would never yield one scrap of Britain's heritage." The Americans made it clear that their proposal "applied only to former League of Nations mandates established after World War I, territories taken from Axis nations during the war [World War II], and any areas which might be voluntarily handed over by colonial Powers to international control" (McNeill 1953, p. 554).

Roosevelt informed Churchill of a conversation with General Chiang Kai-shek in which he had confirmed that the Chinese had no designs on Indo-China because it had a completely different culture. Therefore a trusteeship would be a perfect solution. Churchill responded that it was "nonsense." Roosevelt then replied to the Prime Minister:

> Winston, this is something which you are just not able to understand. You have 400 years of acquisitive instinct in your blood and you just don't understand how a country might not want to acquire land somewhere if they can get it. A new period has opened in the world's history, and you will have to adjust yourself to it (Stettinius 1949, p.237).

Roosevelt said, "the British would take land anywhere in the world even if it were only a rock or a sand bar" (Stettinius 1949, p 237). Stalin agreed that Indo-China should be independent, but he expressed the view that it was not yet prepared yet to govern itself; therefore, Stalin felt a trusteeship was ideal. Churchill objected once again, but this time the President reminded him that he was outvoted. The British were opposed to the American and Soviet ideas of trusteeships, perceiving it as a threat to their colonial possessions. After the Prime Minister finished his discourse, still upset, he could be heard rambling to himself, "never, never, never" (Stettinius 1949, p 237). Stettinius calmed Churchill by explaining to him that the issue of trusteeships had nothing to do with the British Empire, and that the proposed trusteeships dealt only with the League of Nations mandates and territories taken from Axis control. This reiteration partially subdued the British leader, but he was adamant that it be made as clear as possible that the statement on trusteeships did not refer to the British Empire. McNeill (1953, p. 554) writes, "Churchill remained indignant and suspicious. His explosive eloquence gave a dramatic demonstration of the strength of his attachment to the Imperial idea."

Less powerful states, not under colonial domination, must have questioned, if only internally, the hypocrisy of Britain and the France possessing vast colonial empires while co-sponsoring the founding of an organization trumpeting the sovereign equality of all nations. The founding sponsors of the U.N. were in the act of violating the spirit of the organization. The United States publicly opposed colonial policy but had become an imperial power in 1896 after invading the Philippines. The American vision focused on economic domination not territorial acquisition, which differed markedly from the British and the French idea of planting their flags on foreign territories. For Americans, controlling a country economically was more advantageous than having to occupy and subdue it to reap its bounty. Occasionally a country got out of order and refused to subordinate itself, and Washington would find a pretext to use military force to put the situation back into the normal hierarchy, with it giving orders and client states, begrudgingly or not, accepting those demands. In 1945, American elites sought to replace traditional colonialism with American neo-colonialism, and the British were keenly aware of this development. In 1942, the British Colonial Secretary said, "We [the British] should realize that deeply embedded in the mind of most Americans was a fundamental distrust of what the [the Americans] called British Imperialism. ... The only way in which we could remove this deep-seated prejudice would be to invite the co-operation of the United States in the development of colonies after the war" (Clemens 1970, p. 217).

San Francisco

President Roosevelt proposed the name "United Nations," which he had taken from the Declaration by United Nations signed in Washington DC on January 1, 1942. Roosevelt died from a massive cerebral hemorrhage on April 12, 1945, just days before the San Francisco conference began on April 25th. The sponsoring powers welcomed forty-five nations to the San Francisco Conference. Every invitee had declared war on Germany and Japan, although some had done so just months before the conference. Over 850 delegates and their advisors converged on the city by the bay, and combined with the secretariat, the total attendance at the conference was 3,500, with an additional 2,500 media personnel and observers. The San Francisco conference was perhaps the largest conference ever to take place (United Nations Web Services 2005).

A few weeks earlier, the Latin American countries had convened in Chapultepec, Mexico to discuss membership in United Nations and had agreed upon universal membership for Latin America, including membership for Argentina. Nelson Rockefeller, Secretary for Latin American Affairs in the U.S. State Department, attended the meeting and supported a seat for Argentina. In San Francisco the Latin American delegations refused to vote to admit the Soviet republics unless Argentina was added as an original member. Stettinius had attempted to include Argentina at Dumbarton Oaks, but this had been unacceptable to Moscow. Vyacheslav Molotov, the Soviet representative at San Francisco, had opposed Argentina's inclusion on the grounds it still had a "fascist" government. Argentina had entered the war only in March 1945. To the displeasure of the Soviets, Argentina was admitted as an original member, and adding to this aggravation, the Americans refused to grant admittance to the Soviet-backed Lublin Poles.

Washington employed client states to place conditions on agreements reached at Yalta, where, only months earlier, the American delegation had communicated to the Soviets that the Latin American states could not be controlled. However, it was apparent that the United States had excessive influence over their southern neighbors (Hilderbrand 1990, p. 254). The Soviets witnessed a mendacious American plan to dominate the organization unfold. At Yalta the Americans and British had argued for the rights of small states to bring issues to the table for discussion. Stalin had questioned this, believing that small states would desire a favorable decision rather than merely expressing opinions. Washington wanted smaller countries, desirably client states, to do their work by bringing issues to the table for a vote, and to insure a favorable outcome; this strategy applied both to the Security Council and the General Assembly, with the former taking precedent due to its binding nature. Stalin had feared that the Americans would try to isolate the Soviet Union, to produce conditions that would make it vulnerable, and to make it the black sheep in the family of nations, which is exactly the strategy Washington began to implement (Hilderbrand 1990, p. 254). The Soviet leader felt it would be a slippery path if small states were able to divide the unity of the great powers for their own benefit, but the opposite occurred; the United States began to use small states for the benefit of American foreign policy. These divisions and growing distrust festered while the public face of the Great Powers at the San Francisco conference remained unified.

The membership adopted the United Nations Charter on May 24, 1945 and signed it on June 26th. The framers designed the organization so that members would conduct business keeping three key elements in mind: universalism and equality of member states, pre-eminence of the Security Council, and broad mandates and breadth of institutional machinery (Bhatta 2000, p. 35). Positive results hinged on unity and cooperation among nations, especially the most powerful. The unity of the Big Three in the fight against Nazism and fascism and the relative post-war cooperation to establish the United Nations were accomplished in a spirit of mutual understanding; these diplomatic successes in coping with massive crisis proved that in international politics the capacity exists for constructing confidence on the basis of close coinciding interests between states belonging to different social systems (Yakovlev 1985, p. 9).

The Charter enshrined clear privileges for the permanent members over all others signatories, yet this did not block the legitimation of the U.N. at San Francisco. The most plausible explanation for the success of the conference is that states were able to "discuss, criticize, and vote" on the draft charter and that "the deliberative opportunities were crucial to making the conference work, even without a significant chance that they would result in substantive changes to the draft in line with the opponents' proposals" (Hurd 2007, pp. 106-7). On one occasion the sponsors threatened to withdraw from the United Nations project altogether if the membership did not approve the P-5 veto, and they used their advantageous position to formulate a draft and subsequently have it approved without any substantial changes; nevertheless, the sponsors never used overt force to gain approval of the U.N. draft charter, and their adhering to the rules of procedure, which they designed to promote a favorable outcome for their interests, became an important aspect in legitimizing the draft charter and winning the approval of the general membership.[1] If the draft charter had been signed in April

---

1 Twelve technical committees had the responsibility for the most important task: drafting. Where needed, these committees had sub-committees under four general commissions. "All delegations were allowed to be represented in all commissions and committees" (Simma et al. 1994, p. 10). One level higher than the technical committees, just below the Plenary level (the highest level), were four additional committees: a Steering Committee, an Executive Committee, a Coordinating Committee including an Advisory Committee of Jurists, and a Credential Committee. *The Charter of the United Nations: Commentary* notes, "The texts elaborated by the lower committees were passed on to the respective commissions and from there were changed only in exceptional cases upon review by the Coordinating Committee and the Advisory Committee of Jurists" (Simma et al. 1994, p.10). When texts were changed substantially, a rare occurrence, they were returned to the original technical committees. The purpose of this process was to ensure that the proper technical legal wording was used, to check the language, to eliminate contradictions, and to create a uniform terminology. When a text was ready, it had to be cleared by the Coordinating Committee and then the Steering Committee, which was composed of heads of all delegations, before it was sent to the Plenary Assembly for vote and adoption. All sessions of the Plenary and commissions were open to the public, while committee and sub-committees were open only to members of delegations. The San Francisco conference was indeed inclusive and provided all delegations a chance to be play a role in giving birth to the United Nations Charter (Simma et al. 1994, p. 10).

1945 it would have made little to no difference to the text.[2] However, the deliberative process at San Francisco — which allowed delegations to voice opinions, vote, and propose changes — was crucial in legitimating the U.N. among the original signatories because it signified their inclusion in the international community. Hurd (2007, p. 109) writes, "By carefully following the procedures, the strong states grounded their claim that the fight had been properly conducted and the result should therefore be respected."

Small and medium states viewed the ability to bring issues to the table of the Council as useful. Article 35 (1) secured the right of non-Council U.N. members to bring an issue to the Council floor, Article 35 (2) provided the right to entities that are not U.N. members to bring issues to the table, and Article 99 ensured the right of the Secretary General to propose items. The U.N. charter provided the right to bring an issue to the Council, allowing the "little birds to sing" as Churchill had stated at Yalta; however a permanent member could terminate the discussion if unwilling to entertain the issue. Nevertheless, the ability for small and medium states to discuss and vote on the draft Charter and to bring issues to the Council was crucial in the legitimation process.[3]

---

2 The substance of the Charter remained nearly the same. However, as a result of lobbying from Latin American delegates and forty civil society groups in San Francisco, provisions for a human rights commission were included. Also, several women delegates from Latin American lobbied for the inclusion of the phrase "to ensure respect for human rights without distinction as to race, sex, condition or creed" (Krasno 2004, p. 40)

3 Chayes and Chayes (1995) and Franck (1995) are three scholars, among others, who employ the concept of fairness in the process of legitimation. Chayes and Chayes (1995) argue that fairness is a key element in legitimation and that compliance with international norms depends largely on whether or not the norm is viewed as fair. They claim that fairness is a prerequisite to legitimacy. Franck (1995) argues that fairness is a component to legitimacy, but he uses an opposite approach, claiming that the legitimacy of an institution creates the belief that the product is fair. Weber (1968), Habermas (1973), Steffek (2003), and Franck (1990) are among those scholars who argue for a procedural approach to legitimation. In the *Power of Legitimacy among Nations*, Franck (1990, p. 24, 26) writes that an institution establishes its legitimacy when "it has come into being and operates in accordance with general-

Chapter Two: The Security Council

In 2006, Venezuela employed a global campaign to win a two-year Security Council seat. Washington, due to political differences with Caracas, was equally zealous in its opposition. The mass media, including *the Los Angeles Times* and *the Christian Science Monitor*, purported that U.S. opposition stemmed from fear that Venezuela would "interfere with plans" for the U.S. to pressure and possibly sanction Iran. (Reagan 2006). These absurd claims were made in the mainstream American media even though Venezuela was seeking a non-permanent seat, which carries no veto privilege. During

---

ly accepted principles of right process...Legitimacy is that attribute of a rule which conduces to the belief that it is fair because it was made and applied in accordance with right process." Franck (1995, p.30) also acknowledges beyond the procedural approach that the output does play a role in legitimacy, listing "four indications of legitimacy: determinacy, symbolic validation, coherence, and adherence." He believes that the extent to which these four components are adhered to is the extent of the legitimacy of the institution. Regarding Franck's indications relating to the procedural approach, Hurd (2007, p. 70) writes that "it may be very difficult to separate the legitimating effects of 'current' procedures from those of substantive outputs of the institution or process, but conceptually the two are clearly distinct causal mechanisms" Hurd (2007, p. 72).

---

the run up to the First Gulf War in 1990-1991, Cuba and Yemen occupied seats on the Council, and despite opposition and negative votes from both countries — they were ineffectual in stopping the U.S. and its allies from using the Security Council to authorize force against Iraq's incursion into Kuwait. American opposition to a Venezuelan Council seat had more to do with symbolism than substance. Washington did not want to see Hugo Chavez's government secure the legitimacy and prestige that is attached to being voted onto the Security Council by members of the General Assembly.

Washington needed to find an opposition candidate, so it backed Guatemala for the seat and used its soft power to persuade countries to follow suit. The secret ballot made the situation less difficult for third-party states, which could avoid the repercussions of a public vote; however, numerous countries, in both camps, gave verbal commitments. Although denied by the State Department, *The Los Angeles Times* reported that Washington had warned Chilean pilots that they would not be trained to fly the F-16 warplanes — the United States had agreed to sell Chile — if the Chilean government backed Venezuela's campaign (Borger 2006). By close of the first week in September, Guatemalan delegations had "lobbied in 60 capitals," and they anticipated support from "most of Europe as well as some of Asia and Africa" (Katz 2006). Venezuela claimed that it held the Caribbean, Mercosur, Russia, China, and the Arab League.

Hugo Chavez spent millions of dollars campaigning and made state visits to China, Russia, and the Middle East (Brubaker 2006). In 2006, Chavez traveled to more than two dozen countries on five continents, visiting countries multiple times, often issuing statements campaigning for the Security Council seat (*The Economist* Sept. 2006). Chavez's tour was said to range from "modest but symbolic outlays to huge deals sometimes dwarfing U.S. bilateral aid" (Pilkington & Carroll, 2006).

After 47 rounds of voting, the Assembly remained unable to reach the two-thirds majority needed to select the Security Council seat from the Latin American Group. Ultimately, Panama was chosen as a compromise state, a country that could bridge the gap between South and Central America and be acceptable to both Guatemala and Venezuela (*BBC News* 11 Nov. 2006). The intense U.S. lobbying against Venezuela demonstrated two things: first, how seriously the United States is taking Hugo Chavez's oil-rich Venezuela and its rising influence in Latin America, and second, it reaffirmed the legitimacy and symbolic power attached to the United Nations Security Council. Tariq Ali, a noted British journalist, commented on the election: "This would have been a routine vote. It didn't matter to them which Latin American country sits on the Security Council. There's no right to veto. But they are fearful that the Venezuelans will use the Security Council as a platform to put an alternative view forward" (*DemocracyNow.org* 17 Oct. 2006).

Governments make lavish efforts to be elected as non-permanent members of the Security Council. In August 2000, with two months remaining until the election, Ireland's Minister of Foreign Affairs Brian Cowen had already met with 47 member states seeking support for Ireland's candidacy, and in the process the Irish government spent 1.2 million pounds (*Irish Times* 10 Aug. 2000). One would assume the payoff of such intense campaigning would come in the form of increased influence over Council decisions; but nothing could be further from the truth. Non-permanent members on the Council have miniscule influence on decision making, and the influence appropriated to them has been steadily declining. Ironically, the competition for seats has increased.

Ian Hurd (2007) compared the decision-making influence on Council activities of non-permanent members with non-members and found little difference between the two (Hurd 2007, pp. 118-123). He attributes this to changes in the Council's working methods. All members now have some power over shaping the agenda, but more importantly, non-members are routinely invited for private consultations among permanent members based on their material contribution to peacekeeping missions. States that contribute more resources to the U.N., such as Germany and Japan, have developed their own special "quasi-membership" on the Council. These states are often invited for consultations on the Council floor, whether elected or not. The Council regularly conducts consultations with blocks of states such as the Non-Aligned Movement, one third of Council meetings bring non-Council members to participate, and, finally, most of the substantive work takes place between the permanent members during informal discussions. It is interesting to note that in the opening paragraph of the provisional record of almost every Council meeting, the President of the Council says, "The Security Council is meeting in accordance with understanding reached in its prior consultations." Most of the real work gets hammered out behind closed doors between representatives of the permanent members.

Permanent member states that seek authorization to use military force may encounter opposition from one or more veto wielding members of the Council. However, if a non-permanent member objects it may be reprimanded by a dominant power, such as the United States. Yemen voted against authorizing force against Iraq in 1991, and a U.S. representative, within earshot of a microphone, told Yemen's ambassador, "That will be the most expensive no vote you ever cast" (Atkinson & Gellman 1991, p. A1). This quote, which appeared in a published report, was "not disputed by the U.S. State Department" (Atkinson & Gellman, 1991, p. A1). The U.S. quickly punished Yemen: "In the following days, thousands of Yemeni laborers were deported from Saudi Arabia, and the United States cut off a 70 million aid package [all U.S. aid to Yemen]" (Lynch 2002, p. A24). The Yemenis' vote had no material effect on the resolution to use force against Iraq, but perhaps the United States desired a unanimous vote or simply would not tolerate dissent.

The pressure applied on smaller and medium size Council member states to vote affirmatively for a resolution of importance to a powerful permanent member, especially an economic power, fosters a situation in which brute strength can dominate principled votes. The economic strength of permanent members and their relative immunity from coercion contributes to their ability to vote independently. A Harvard study found that "on average, the typical developing country serving on the council can anticipate an additional $16 million from the United States," and during "important years," the number rises to "$45 million from the United States" (Kuziemko & Werker 2006, p. 924). Smaller countries do vote on principle, but there have been many instances when they have had their votes compromised by economic incentives or have been punished economically for voting against a powerful state's agenda, therefore, it remains imperative to have veto wielding members that are economically independent powers.

The Security Council Veto

From 1945 to 1965, the Soviet Union was responsible for 95 percent of all vetoes.[4] The large number of Soviet vetoes and the lack of a single U.S. veto are misleading. Moscow's veto did not have a great effect on preventing action or on weakening the organization, instead, to a certain degree, the Soviet veto strengthened it. The Soviet veto had one of three fates: it "stuck," was circumvented, or was superseded by direct negotiation between the disputants and because the circumstances changed the dispute was resolved.[5]

Whether or not the United States and the Western powers chose to circumvent the Soviet veto largely depended on the beneficiary. In the first twenty years, the Soviet Union had greater success in direct confrontations with the United States and on proxy vetoes cast on behalf of neutral states than on defending communist

---

4 In the first two decades of the United Nations, the Soviet Union exercised its veto 103 times; France, 4 times; the United Kingdom, 3 times; and China, once. The United States did not exercise its veto.

5 When a Soviet veto stuck no further action was taken by states or other UN organs; for example, the case with the Soviet veto of the investigation of the Indian invasion of Goa in 1961. The Soviet veto of the 'liberation" of Goa stuck, not because of a lack of "alternative machinery that might have been used against it," but because the United States was aware that they did not possess sufficient votes in the GA to bypass the veto (Stoessinger 1977, p. 11). It became clear that the GA would vote in favor of the Soviet position because the situation was a case of an Indian "liberation" and not a case of Indian "aggression" as the West perceived it. The Soviet veto acted as a statement of the majority view instead of a means to block the majority. When a Soviet veto was "circumvented," the case was diverted to another UN organ, which provided alternative machinery; for example, the General Assembly circumvented the Soviet veto of the "police action" in Korea.

allied states. From 1945 to 1965, 35 percent of vetoes cast in direct confrontations against the United States stuck, and 40 percent of vetoes cast on behalf of neutral states stuck while only 12 percent of vetoes cast on behalf of communist allies stuck (Stoessinger 1977, p. 11). The United States and other U.N. members acknowledged that in direct confrontations between the superpowers the reality of power had to be accepted and that pushing too hard could cause a rupture capable of breaking the United Nations. Instead, the superpowers fought through proxy states, which made conflict within the U.N. less likely to result in a shattering of the organization from excessive pressure. Cold War politics played a central role in the use of the veto and U.N. Security Council Strategy, and until 1990, the United States remained reluctant to circumvent Soviet vetoes supporting neutralist states, because of the risk of pushing them into the Soviet camp. Both superpowers were eager to gain neutralist support. However, the United States, which bypassed five vetoes during the Korean War, had no qualms circumventing vetoes that were cast on behalf of the Soviet Union's communist allies. All together, the permanent members cast 199 vetoes between 1946 and 1989, which averages to more than 4 vetoes per year. Between 1990 and 2007, the official use of the veto lessened dramatically, with only 21 vetoes cast, an average of about one veto per year.

The Security Council Summary Statement or "Agenda"[6] is comprised of two parts: the provisional agenda and the Summary State-

---

6 In early 2005, the Summary Statement had 147 items listed, dating as far back to a few years after the U.N.'s founding (Hurd 2007, p. 113). In 1996, the Security Council, without consulting the general membership, made an effort to reform how the Summary Statement functioned by establishing a procedural rule that stated, "Matters that had not been considered by the Council in the preceding five years would be deleted from the list of matters of which the Council was seized" (United Nations 1997) After the passage of this rule, 42 out of the 139 items on the Summary Statement were set for deletion. Intense opposition by non-Council members forced a compromise amendment, allowing UN members to retain items on the Summary Statement by formally notifying the Secretary General; in that case, the item would remain on the list for a year, with the one-year deferment being "indefinitely renewable" (Hurd 2007, p. 115). In early 1997, 29 of 42 items that were eligible to be cut remained on the list. In October 1997, five

items were deleted and one item was preserved by appeal. As 1997 came to a close, the Summary Statement, including new items, still had 128 items (Hurd 2007, p. 115). In early 2005, the Summary Statement had 147 items listed, dating as far back to a few years after the U.N.'s founding (Hurd 2007, p. 113). In 1996, the Security Council, without consulting the general membership, made an effort to reform how the Summary Statement functioned by establishing a procedural rule that stated, "Matters that had not been considered by the Council in the preceding five years would be deleted from the list of matters of which the Council was seized" (United Nations 1997). After the passage of this rule, 42 out of the 139 items on the Summary Statement were set for deletion. Intense opposition by non-Council members forced a compromise amendment, allowing UN members to retain items on the Summary Statement by formally notifying the Secretary General; in that case, the item would remain on the list for a year, with the one-year deferment being "indefinitely renewable" (Hurd 2007, p. 115). In early 1997, 29 of 42 items that were eligible to be cut remained on the list. In October 1997, five items were deleted and one item was preserved by appeal. As 1997 came to a close, the Summary Statement, including new items, still had 128 items (Hurd 2007, p. 115).

The India–Pakistan dispute is one of the longest running disputes since the UN's inception, and Pakistan often references the Summary Statement in its public statements in an effort to garner increased attention for the issue. In October 1998, a Pakistani spokesperson said that the dispute was "the oldest issue on the UN agenda" (*Radio Pakistan* 6 Oct. 1998). The India-Pakistan dispute dates to January 6, 1948, while the introduction of the Palestinian question came on December 9, 1947, but, due to postponement, was only discussed on February 24, 1948. The Palestinian question still remains on the agenda; therefore, the Pakistani spokesperson was only partially correct in citing the India-Pakistan dispute as "the oldest issue on the UN agenda" (United Nations 1966). Nevertheless, Pakistan has sought to gain greater notice at the UN for the dispute. The Deputy Permanent Representative of Pakistan to the UN, Khalid Aziz Baber, declared on Radio Pakistan that the dispute in Jammu and Kashmir "deserved a more detailed reference in the UN Secretary General's annual report" (*Radio Pakistan* 6 Oct. 1998). Islamabad has been very diligent in assuring that items concerning its dispute with India never get deleted from the Summary Statement. This watchful dedication to maintain its issue on the Summary Statement led Pakistan to submit its request 14 months before the deadline for the January 1999 statement (Hurd 2007, p. 116). Securing an item on the agenda produces no concrete benefits for that particular issue, and there is close to no hope of that item resurfacing for substantive discussion at a Council meeting, but, despite this reality, governments find that the benefit of having an item on the Agenda ment. Before each Council meeting, the Secretary General organizes the provisional agenda — a list of issues to be addressed. Council members discuss and vote to approve the provisional agenda, as the "official agenda." The second part of the agenda, the Summary Statement, is an ongoing list of issues that have been discussed and could be reopened for further deliberation. The Council may also wish to suspend conversation on an issue but not want to formally close the matter. It is worth noting that an issue placed on the Summary Statement rarely reemerges on the Council floor for any meaningful consideration.

Permanent members control the agenda through the use of the hidden veto. Restricted topics, such as Afghanistan and Iraq, are off-limits. The use of the hidden veto in blocking discussion of those topics is well known by elected members of the Council, who quickly learn the Council's informal rules of procedure. The United States often uses its veto, hidden or real, to shield Israel from Security Council condemnation. In February 2011, President Obama used his first Security Council veto to block condemnation of illegal Israeli settlements in Palestinian territories. The U.S. was the only negative vote among the fifteen members and the draft had over 100 co-sponsors and garnered the support of over 130 countries. The United States, acting against the will of the international community, has used its veto power more than forty times to shield Israel from official Security Council condemnation for its crimes against the Palestinian people.

"Uniting For Peace"

The General Assembly adopted Resolution 377 "Uniting for Peace" on November 3, 1950. The United States had proposed it to the GA to circumvent Soviet vetoes of military action in Korea. Invoking the resolution transfers a case to the General Assembly

---

is their issue's association with the universal legitimacy of the United Nations. This mere association reaps positive rewards by signaling the seriousness and international scope of a particular issue, causing third-party states to give closer attention to an issue because of its connection to the symbolic power of the "Official Agenda."

through the creation of an emergency special session (ESS), which can be established with a procedural vote from the Security Council or by a request from the majority of members of the United Nations. "Uniting for Peace" has been invoked ten times, mostly by the United States. In 1956, after Egyptian President Gamal Abdel Nasser nationalized the Suez Canal, Britain, France, and Israel invaded Egypt. President Eisenhower demanded a halt to the invasion and called for a cease-fire, but Britain and France vetoed cease-fire resolutions in the Council. Under "Uniting for Peace an emergency session of the GA convened and a resolution passed that resulted in Britain and France withdrawing from Egypt inside a week.[7]

The constitutionality of the resolution, under the Charter, has been called into question because of the Security Council's role as identifier of threats to international peace and security. The Charter states that the Council has the "primary" responsibility for peace and security and Resolution 377 and this phrasing opened the possibility that the GA may play an alternate role if the Council was unable to fulfill its responsibility. "Uniting for Peace" was adopted to demonstrate the international community's resolve to act when the Council is unable or unwilling. In 1950, when the resolution came into effect, the world remained under the dark cloud of colonialism, with only fifty nine countries comprising the GA, a majority unduly influenced by Washington. Today, with 194 member states, the makeup of the GA accurately represents the interna-

---

7 GA Res. 377A (1) explains the purpose of the resolution: Resolves that if the Security Council, because of lack of unanimity of permanent members, fails to exercise its primary responsibility for the maintenance of peace and security in any case where there appears to be a threat to the peace, breach of the peace, or act of aggression, the General Assembly shall consider the matter immediately with a view to making appropriate recommendations to Members for collective measures, including in the case of a breach of the peace or act of aggression the use of armed forces when necessary, to maintain or restore international peace and security. If not in session at the time, the General Assembly may meet in emergency special session within twenty-four hours of the request therefor. Such emergency special session shall be called if requested by the Security Council on the vote of any seven members, or by a majority of the Members of the United Nations (United Nations 1950, sect. A.1).

tional community and "Uniting for Peace" is an option available to the international community to address threats to global peace and security.

The General Assembly has the capacity to establish subsidiary organs and under "Uniting for Peace" an alternate body can be established when the Council has failed to fulfill its duties under the Charter; in such a case the Peace Observation Commission is given the authority to exercise the functions of the Security Council.[8] The International Court of Justice (ICJ) has validated the legitimacy of the resolution by referring to it in its rulings and acknowledging that it is constitutionally valid. One such ruling was the July 9, 2004, advisory opinion on the "Legal Consequences of the Construction of a Wall in the Occupied Territory" (ICJ 2004, pp. 1-4). In the ICJ ruling, the court again acknowledged that the General Assembly acted *ultra vires* under the U.N. Charter in convening the Tenth Emergency Special Session and continuing to act under that session (ICJ 2004, p. 2). Action does not necessarily mean "enforcement action," but the authorization of an emergency GA session is a statement by the international community that the Council has failed to fulfill its duty and that something will be done within the legitimacy of the United Nations to address the immediate problem. In the case of the Israeli fence, the continuous use of the veto by the United States to oppose any resolution condemning Israel led the ICJ to rule that invoking Res. 377 "Uniting for Peace" was ultra vires.

A veto in response to a draft resolution calling for coercive measures may be permanent members acting in the best interest of peace and upholding the principles of the United Nations. The facts

---

8 GA Resolution 377 section B.3 established the Peace Observation Commission: "...Upon invitation or with the consent of the State into whose territory the Commission would go, the General Assembly, or the Interim Committee when the Assembly is not in session, may utilize the Commission if the Security Council is not exercising the functions assigned to it by the Charter with respect to the matter in question. Decisions to utilize the Commission shall be made on the affirmative vote of two-thirds of the members present and voting. The Security Council may also utilize the Commission in accordance with its authority under the Charter (United Nations 1950, sect. B.3).

on the ground, validated as widely as possible to include consent from dominant and subordinate actors, should determine whether a threat to international peace and security exists.

The most glaring issue concerning the veto, and the Security Council generally, even more troublesome than Washington's misuse of its privilege to shield Israel from condemnation or the lack of democratic participation by the general membership, is the disregard for the value of the veto when it poses an obstacle to American or Western military intervention. In a September 23rd, 2007, interview with Tim Russert on *Meet the Press*, Hillary Clinton expressed the traditional U.S. government attitude toward the United Nations most accurately; the Senator said, "I don't believe it's in the best interests of our country to give the United Nations what amounts to a veto over presidential action. I think that the Congress and the president should determine what presidential action should be" (*MSNBC.com*, 27 September 2007).

The United States and North Atlantic Treaty Organization (NATO) governments, desiring to be viewed as pursuing legitimate international policies, have invented rationales to secure the perception of legality. In 1980, the Security Council drafted a resolution calling for sanctions against Iran because of the U.S. hostage situation in that country and it was vetoed by the Soviet Union.[9]

---

9 The U.S. tabled this resolution to follow up resolution 461, adopted on December 31, 1979, that stated (in paragraph 6), "in order to review the situation and, in the event of non-compliance with this resolution, to adopt effective measures under Articles 39 and 41 of the Charter of the United Nations." The resolution was vetoed by the USSR. Subsequent to that veto, U.S. Ambassador to the United Nations, Donald McHenry, spoke to the Council about implementing a vetoed resolution based on a previous resolution (Res. 46): "under resolution 461 (1979) the Council undertook a binding obligation to adopt effective measures and under Article 25 of the Charter all Member States are obliged to respect the provisions of resolution 461 (1979). The Soviet veto now attempts to block the membership from fulfilling that obligation. The question then arises what a member bound by resolution 461 (1979) and acting in good faith pursuant to its obligations under Article 2 (2) of the Charter, should do to implement that resolution.... [T]he membership of the United States at large remains obligated to review the situation and the event of Iran's non-compliance with it, an event that

The United States and Europe sought to create legitimacy for sanctions by associating their positions and actions with vetoed draft Resolution S/13735. On April 7, 1980, after diplomatic relations between Iran and the United States had already been severed, President Jimmy Carter stated that he would proceed with a number of actions against Iran and its nationals, citing S/13735, the vetoed resolution, in order to gain more authority for the implementation of programs against Iran.[10] The European Common Market Ministers (ECMFM) followed Washington's lead and used S/13735 to support the President's actions and to request that European national parliaments implement a program of sanctions against Iran. The European Common Market Ministers (ECMFM) adopted a resolution on April 22, 1980, using the vetoed resolution to gain authority for such action.[11] The ECMFM's statement implied "that the vetoed resolution is, with 'the rules of international law,' a coequal basis for the contemplated sanctions program" (Reisman 1980, p. 905).[12] Al-

has come to pass, and to take effective measures consistent with the Charter to implement that resolution" (Reisman 1980, p. 904-5).

10 President Carter stated, "[T]he Secretary of the Treasury will put into effect official sanctions prohibiting exports from the United States to Iran, in accordance with the sanctions approved by 10 members of the United Nations Security Council on January 13 in the resolution which was vetoed by the Soviet Union" (Reisman 1980, p. 905).

11 Paragraph 5 of that resolution stated: "The Foreign Ministers of the Nine, deeply concerned that a continuation of this situation may endanger international peace and security, have decided to request their national Parliaments immediately to take any necessary measures to impose sanctions against Iran in accordance with the Security Council resolution on Iran of 10 January 1980, which was vetoed, and in accordance with the rules of international law" (Reisman 1980, p. 905). Paragraph five referred to the vetoed UN resolution to support the American sanctions proposal.

12 Reisman (1980, p. 905) argues that if the European Ministers felt they already possessed the authority to impose sanctions on Iran, then citing a terminated resolution was perplexing: "If the Ministers' view was that a Security Council resolution was not needed for the initiation of trade and other export controls by one or more states against another state engaged in serious and continuing violation of international law, then the reference to the vetoed resolution was gratuitous and confusing." The ECMFM had its reasoning for using the language it did. Reisman (1980, p. 906) adds, "If their [ECMFM] view was that the Charter and

though President Carter employed language more nuanced than the European Ministers' words, Carter also implied that an otherwise illegal action had gained certain legality because of the affirmative vote of ten members on the Security Council. He implied that there was legal authority in vetoed Resolution S/13735. The United States and NATO governments used the veto resolution in an attempt to create a perception of legality.

The 1999 U.S.–NATO attack on the Federal Republic of Yugoslavia (FRY), which will be discussed in depth in a later chapter, bypassed Russian and Chinese opposition and brushed aside the significance of the veto. Moscow and Beijing experienced disrespect and felt Washington and NATO governments were attempting to render their permanent role on the Council as worthless. Carpenter (2000, p. 77) writes, "Possession of a veto power as permanent members of the Security Council would have little relevance if the United States and its allies could simply ignore the Council's prerogative to approve or reject proposals to use coercive measures and act on their own." The Russian Prime Minister, Yevgeny Primakov, was en route over the Atlantic to high level talks in Washington, DC, when he received word that NATO was going through with its military operations against the FRY; he promptly had the plane turn around in mid-flight. The Russian government, outraged at the U.S.–NATO attack, recalled its military officers serving in liaison capacities at NATO in Brussels and expelled NATO officers from Russia (Carpenter 2000, pp. 78-79).

international law require Council authorization for such sanctions, the invocation of a vetoed resolution may have had more significant legal implications."

CHAPTER THREE: ALTERNATIVE NORM JUSTIFICATIONS

Two widely used alternative norms exist: humanitarian intervention and self-defense. While legitimate cases of self-defense and humanitarian rescue exist, they are few in comparison with cases of aggression justified by these alternative norms.

Defining humanitarian intervention is uncontroversial. Stowell (1983, p. 53) provides an accepted definition: "the reliance upon the use of force for the justifiable purpose of protecting the inhabitants of another state from treatment which is so arbitrarily and persistently abusive as to exceed the limits of that authority within which the sovereign is presumed to act with reason and justice." What is contested is under what circumstances forcible intervention should be pursued, if at all. Three commonly held positions on humanitarian intervention exist: absolute non-interventionism, limited interventionism, and broad interventionism (Tesón 1997, p. 23-24). Non-interventionists argue that the use of force is only justified when thwarting aggression. Limited interventionists argue that forcible intervention is justifiable in the instance of extreme humanitarian cases, such as acts of genocide. Broad interventionists, who favor unilateral action to react forcibly, when desirable, without having to achieve a consensus among nations, argue for the use of force against states that violate human rights even if those violations are not extreme. For the broad interventionist, respecting the norm of non-intervention in the face of a tyrant's oppression of his own people is tantamount to the absurd, while limited interventionists point to cases such as genocide in Rwanda in 1994 to argue for the necessity to respond with the use of force but only under extreme circumstances.

Non-interventionists cite ample documentation that demonstrates the necessity to respect the norms of non-interference, territorial integrity, and the sovereignty of states. All three positions claim to be legitimate; however, real legitimacy is based on the law, shared beliefs, and consent from relevant subordinate actors; it is not based on the powerful state's ability to influence domestic or international public opinion.

Article 2(4) of the U.N. Charter prohibits the use of force: "All Members shall refrain in their international relations from the threat or use of force against the territorial integrity or political independence of any state, or in any other manner inconsistent with the Purposes of the United Nations" (United Nations 2003a, p. 6). Scholars and analysts arguing in favor of unilateral humanitarian intervention have used a narrow interpretation of Article 2(4) to attempt to provide legal backing for their position, claiming that if the Charter had intended to prohibit all force that crosses territorial boundaries it would have explicitly said so. According to this argument, instances of force exist that fail to meet the level of force described in Article 2(4) yet are consistent with the U.N. Charter; therefore, it is argued, such interventions are legal under the Charter. This point of view also maintains that, in a humanitarian intervention, the use of force "does not result in territorial conquest, political subjugation, or any other challenge to the territorial integrity or political independence of the target state" (Falk 1996, p. 37). Professor Emeritus in International Law at Princeton University Richard Falk (1996) explains this narrow interpretation of Article 2(4) in his study on the legality of 'humanitarian intervention':

> Thus, it is alleged to articles 1(3), 55, 56, and the preamble of the Charter, in combination with specific human rights instru-

ments, that the "co-equal" value of the ban of force and universal respect for, and observance of, human rights and "fundamental freedoms" (article 55) implies the legality of humanitarian intervention. In this view, then the advent of the United Nation [sic] neither terminated nor weakened the customary institution of humanitarian intervention and it said that the use of force for the protection of human rights, far from being inconsistent with the purpose of the United Nations, is rather in conformity with the most fundamental preemptory norms of the Charter (Falk 1996, p. 38).

Scholars adhering to the prohibition of force and taking a broad interpretation of 2(4) find fault with these arguments. The broad interpretation of 2(4) interprets the terms "territorial integrity" and "political independence" as meaning "territorial inviolability," and it interprets the latter half of Article 2(4) as having no effect on the complete prohibition of the use of force. However, Falk (1996, p. 38) argues that "it is unrealistic to assume that an entire population can be rescued from systematic persecution without changing the government or legal status of the territory inhabited by the persecuted population."

Falk (1996, p. 98) concludes in his study that the unilateral use of force for humanitarian intervention is "in contravention of Article 2(4) of the U.N. Charter, broadly construed," but a "de facto" right exists for the Security Council to authorize humanitarian intervention as a collective action. Article 2(7) clearly states that the principle of interfering in the domestic jurisdiction of any state "shall not prejudice the application of enforcement measures under Chapter VII" (United Nations 2003a, p. 7). Those enforcement actions must be consistent with the principles of the United Nations and international law. This does not necessarily mean that the Security Council has the right to intervene in the domestic jurisdiction of any state where there are human rights abuses. Using a hypothetical example, the Security Council should not intervene with collective military action if there are clear cases of epidemic police brutality in New York City. This matter falls under domestic jurisdiction of the United States government, and any forcible intervention would create a much worse human rights situation and an increase in suffering from the violent conflict and its repercussions.

Beckman (2005, p. 35) argues, in regard to humanitarian intervention, that "there seems to be an increasing tendency to discuss issues of general legitimacy parallel with matters of legality without making sufficient distinction." Of course, there is a distinction between the two terms. Legality is a component of legitimacy; legitimacy is therefore a broader concept than legality. However, without legality there is no legitimacy.[13]

Weber's flawed conception relegates legitimacy to the most powerful to convince the subordinate. Beetham (1991, p. 8) argues that social scientists that use the Weberian conception of legitimacy "become skeptical about the possibility of any rational grounding for normative ideas or value systems." Social scientists holding this view tend to favor polling and statistical data and have accepted that a "belief" that something is legitimate makes it so. However, basing legitimacy solely on the belief of people, who may have a variety of motives and biases and are subject to manipulation, is not a tenable position.

Former U.N. Assistant Secretary General Ramesh Thakur (2006, pp. 8-9) writes, "What distinguishes rule enforcement by criminal thugs from that by police officers is legitimacy." Again, power is legitimated and becomes legitimate authority when three conditions are met: "its conformity to established rules; the justifiability of the rules by reference to shared beliefs; the express consent of the subordinate, or the most significant among them to the particular relations of power" (Beetham 1991, p. 19). The degree to which these conditions are met determines the degree of legitimacy. Legitimacy is not an "all or nothing affair" (Beetham 1991, p. 19-20). However, conformity to established rules is requisite; otherwise, the result can only be illegitimate. Unilateral "humanitarian intervention" remains illegal, under any reading of the U.N. Charter.

---

13 This takes into account that laws must also be legitimate: consisting of a minimum level of shared beliefs between relevant dominant and subordinate actors and consent from the subordinate.

The use of collective humanitarian intervention poses significant challenges. First, the Security Council applies its judgments with inconsistency and selectivity: condemning some, ignoring others, and refusing to censure strong allies. Second, the United Nations does not have the resources to engage in humanitarian intervention worldwide. Intervention requires financial and military resources and states willing to sacrifice for a mission. Last and most importantly, the notion of a humanitarian war is contradictory. To bomb and invade a country in order to "free" a population from a tyrant usually results in a humanitarian nightmare. Some scholars arguing for humanitarian intervention paint a situation in which there are two options: to act with military force or to do nothing. This is a false choice. The purpose of the United Nations is to solve crises through peaceful means and diplomacy. The use of incentives and positive diplomacy is far too often overlooked in addressing human right situations, especially in the aftermath of September 11, 2001. The conclusion of Falk (1996) is correct: unilateral intervention for humanitarian reasons is illegal and collective action authorized by the Security Council is legal but should only be used as a last resort. Genocide and mass starvation are examples of situations in which authorization by the Security Council for collective humanitarian intervention by a U.N. commanded force is justified.

In February 2011 — following the mass movement in Egypt that led to the end of Hosni Mubarak's 30 year U.S. supported dictatorship — protests erupted in oil-rich Libya. While some peaceful demonstrations took place, the situation differed markedly from Egypt. Since the outset, the Libyan uprising had the makings of violent insurrection.[14] Pro-Gaddafi forces repelled the armed rebels, who oddly had training and support from Western intelligence agencies and were also reportedly linked to al-Qaeda. Amidst threats from Gaddafi to completely crush the insurrection, the U.S. and NATO called for "humanitarian" no fly zones for the purported

---

14 Richard Falk states the Libyan opposition was "violent from the start and was more in nature of a traditional insurrection against the established order than a popular revolution inspired by democratic values" (Marquand 2011).

benefit of civilians. The U.N. Security Council passed Resolution 1973 to authorize the zones. The resolution also reiterated commitment to the international arms embargo (Resolution 1970) on the whole of Libya.

On March 19, 2011, the U.S. and NATO launched a bombing campaign that punished Tripoli and other population centers. They also were actively violating the arms embargo by funneling weapons to the rebels. Civilian casualties mounted and reports surfaced of the U.S. and NATO using missiles and bombs containing depleted uranium. Russia, China, India, most of South America, the African Union condemned the indiscriminate bombing of Libya. The Arab league backtracked from its initial support for the use of force to implement no-fly zones and condemned the bombing campaign. The U.S. and NATO violated Resolution 1973 and used the no-fly zone justification to obtain a Security Council resolution authorizing force in an attempt to ouster Gaddafi to re-colonize Libya. Regime change became the goal as Hilary Clinton regularly demanded that Gaddafi step down or be overthrown. On April 30, a NATO air strike killed Gaddafi's son and three grandchildren. Four months later, still carrying out massive air strikes, NATO bombed Libyan state television. On August 8, NATO fired missiles on a group of farm buildings in the village of Majar and reportedly killed 85 civilians: 33 children, 32, women, and 20 men. Moussa Ibrahim, spokesman for the Libyan government said, "This is a crime beyond imagination. Everything about this place is civilian" (Sky News 2011). NATO denied that it was targeting civilians. However, shortly after the bombing began, images surfaced in the international media of Libyan children being removed from rubble, although largely ignored by mainstream media in the United States. It became clear, even to those who naively believed the U.S.-NATO rhetoric of "humanitarian intervention," that Western countries had created a humanitarian crisis in Libya while citing "humanitarianism" as an alternative norm justification.

On October 20, 2011, a U.S. Predator drone and a French Mirage jet bombed a convoy of vehicles which were fleeing Sirte. The strike wounded Gaddafi and he fled on foot, only to be captured by rebel forces and, as all evidence suggests, summarily executed. On October 22, Christof Heyns, the U.N. Special Rapporteur on extrajudicial, summary or arbitrary executions, called for an international investigation, stating, "The Geneva Conventions are very clear that when prisoners are taken they may not be executed willfully and if that was the case then we are dealing with a war crime, something that should be tried" (Aljazeera 22 Oct. 2011). On hearing of Gaddafi's death, Secretary of State Hillary Clinton told a CBS reporter, "We came, we saw, he died," and then she laughed (Daly 2011). As the U.S. and NATO ended their military campaign, Mustafa Abdul-Jalil, Libya's interim leader, announced that Sharia law will be the "basic source" of legislation and that any law that "violates Sharia is null and void." The interim leader and governing council lifted, by decree, the ban on polygamy, giving a man the right to take four wives. The abolishment of the marriage law eliminated the right of a woman to keep her home in the case of divorce. As these developments unfolded, the new government, or its supporters, hoisted the black flag of al-Qaeda above the courthouse in Benghazi, a building that was "used by rebel forces to establish their provisional government and media centre" (Greenhill 2011).

States possessing sufficient power to conduct unilateral "humanitarian interventions" still find it a necessity to issue constant justification. Power needs legitimacy to be an authority. Government is based on authority and, therefore, justifications must accompany actions, especially military actions that risk or entail high financial and human costs. This is especially true in democratic nations; however, governments' justifying military actions is universally practiced by both democratic and autocratic governments. Explanations from an autocratic government for a military operation may be addressed to other nations or its own relevant subordinate domestic actors, such as military commanders or soldiers. Governments, almost without exception, provide explanations to justify asking their militaries to go to war. Rulers cannot resort to displays of military power merely because they desire to do so. However, if a state chooses such a rare path, it would be labeled a pariah by the international community and in the case of an autocratic government risk a domestic fracture. No matter the self-interest involved in military intervention, ruling elites always offer an altruistic or noble rationale for war.

Self Defense

Article 2(4):

> All Members shall refrain in their international relations from the threat or use of force against the territorial integrity or political independence of any state, or in any other manner inconsistent with the Purposes of the United Nations (United Nations 2003a, p. 6).

Article 51:

> Nothing in the present Charter shall impair the inherent right of individual or collective self-defense if an armed attack occurs against a Member of the United Nations, until the Security Council has taken the measures necessary to maintain international peace and security. Measures taken by members in the exercise of this right of self-defense shall be immediately reported to the Security Council and shall not in any way affect the authority and responsibility of the Security Council under the present Charter to take at any time such action as it deems necessary in order to maintain or restore international peace and security (United Nations 2003a, pp. 32-33).

Since the beginning of the era of decolonization, governments have used the justification of self-defense as a legal argument, pursuing legal cover and legitimacy for armed interventions. Since 1960, states have repeatedly used the justification of self-defense, invoking it more than any other argument (Beckman 2005, p. 292). They have claimed self defense to justify military interventions for the "protection of own nations, in situations of purported requests rendering it unnecessary, against illegitimate government, for restoration of democracy, against unspecified aggression, as defense against civil invasion by refugees, and to justify preventative intervention to counter non-imminent threats" (Beckman 2005, p. 292). Such a wide variety of justifications, under the heading of self-defense, brings us to two important questions: Do state actors use self-defense as a legal escape clause when there is no coherent legal argument for the use of force? Did the international community intend to make self-defense such a broad concept capable of justifying nearly any imaginable action? The authors of the U.N. Charter did not intend for the self-defense clause under Article 51 to be all inclusive; otherwise, they would not have made Article 51 an "exception" to the prohibition of the use of force. The very notion of an "exception" implies that the concept has a narrow interpretation.

Debate on the preemptive use of force increased in the aftermath of the 2003 U.S. and British invasion of Iraq. In scholarly literature, writers split into two camps regarding interpretation of Article 51 of the U.N. Charter, consisting of "restrictionists" and "counter-restrictionists." Restrictionists claim that the "intent of Article 51 was to limit the use of force in self-defense to those circumstances in which an armed attack has actually occurred" (Arendt 2003, p. 92). On the other hand, the "counter-restrictionists" argue that Article 51 was not intended to restrict what some scholars claim is a "preexisting customary right of self-defense" (Arendt 2003, p. 92). The restrictionist argument is correct in that anticipatory self-defense is not a legal argument. For example, the Japanese stated in 1941 that their attack on Pearl Harbor was an act of self-defense because they had information the United States was preparing to strike Japan and enter the war (Schlesinger, A 2003). Under the counter-restrictionist argument, the Japanese were acting legally in committing what they argued to be a pre-emptive strike. Nevertheless, to present only these two conflicting arguments creates a situation in which two stark choices are envisioned: waiting for an entity or state to strike first and absorbing a first blow before defending oneself or attacking first with a pre-emptive strike. Counter-restrictionists believe in pre-emptive action; however, under such a conception, the target state can claim self-defense for a strike in response to the anticipated pre-emptive attack. And one can see how tangled and absurd this viewpoint can become.

The United Nations has two exceptions to the prohibition of the use of force: collective action authorized by the Security Council (in rare cases the GA via Res. 377) and self-defense under Article 51. States have historically attempted to take advantage of Article 51 by expanding the meaning of *self-defense* to exaggerated levels never intended by the framers of the U.N. Charter. Nevertheless, Article 51 clearly provides a legitimate "exception" to use unilateral proportioned force to repel an immediate attack. The "High-Level Panel on Threats, Challenges and Change," submitted its recommendations to the Secretary General on December 1, 2004. Article 185 of the report addressed the nature of Article 51:

> Article 51 of the U.N. Charter allows States the right of individual or collective self defense. However, section 185 specifies that "a threatened State, according to long established international law, can take military action as long as the threatened attack is imminent, no other means would deflect it, and the action is proportionate. The problem arises when the threat in question is not imminent but still claimed to be true." The Panel importantly recommends, however, that the decision should not be made by the individual state, nor any coalition of States, but should rather be presented to the Security Council for its judgment (Wells 2005, p. 170).[15]

Article 51 should be read in concert with Article 2(4) in order to understand its intended application. The scopes of Article 51 and Article 2(4) are notably different; the latter proscribes "the use of force," and the former addresses the right of self-defense "if an armed attack occurs." An "armed attack" is much narrower than "the use of force."

Two notable approaches have attempted "to deny the lacuna arising from the lack of conformity of Article 2(4) and Article 51" (Simma et al. 1994, p. 664). The perspective that results from these approaches is that a state may respond to any use of force by citing self-defense. However, the wording in the provisions does not support this conclusion.

The first approach views Article 2(4) as proscribing only the use of force that is on the same scale as an "armed attack" referred to in Article 51. The scale of this type of attack would be "substan-

---

15 In 2003, during the General Assembly, Secretary General Kofi Annan requested the creation of a panel to assess the contemporary threats to international peace and security.

tial" and with "considerable effect" (Simma et al. 1994, p. 664).[16] A state that is the victim of a small scale use of force that is below the threshold of an "armed attack" could respond with a similar level of defensive force. However, under this approach, the state initiating force under the threshold would not have committed a violation of Article 2(4), because the level of force was below the threshold of an "armed attack," which would be the level to qualify an act as "the use of force." This approach also fails to take into account that self-defense is usually understood to be a response to an unlawful act. Therefore, defensive force might be justified by claiming that the initiating state had violated some other principle or law such as non-intervention or the respect for another nation's sovereignty.[17]

The second approach views an "armed attack" in an unrestricted sense compared to the prohibition of the use of force referred to

---

16 Since 1950, the International Law Commission, among others, has attempted to reach a consensus on the definition of aggression. The General Assembly adopted Resolution 3314 on December 14, 1974, which provided a definition of "aggression." However, the resolution is a GA resolution, and therefore, it is considered merely a recommendation and not legally binding. In the committee that worked on the definition, the United States and other Western states opposed notions of including the term "armed attack." The United States and the Soviet Union stated that an "act of aggression" and an "armed attack" are not the same. The terms "aggression" and "armed attack" are not the same because an "armed attack" has a narrower definition.

17 The argument that the right of self-defense, under Article 51, exists against small scale attacks because the Charter would permit force below the threshold of an armed attack is unconvincing. In *the United Nations Charter: A Commentary*, it is argued that this line of reasoning could equally claim that "by deliberately not pronouncing upon the small-scale use of force in the content of self-defense and by allowing self-defense in response to an armed attack, the UN Charter had indirectly expressed that no forcible self-defense is permissible against the former" (Simma et al. 1994, p. 665). The *Commentary* continues by arguing that this approach is "superfluous" because it returns to the question of whether, and to what extent, there is a general right of self-defense apart from Article 51..." (Simma et al. 1994, p. 665). The *Commentary* also claims that this approach is "untenable" because it violates the unambiguous words of the Charter and its distinct wording intended to ban the unilateral use of force as much as possible (Simma et al. 1994, p. 665).

---

in Article 2(4). This approach allows self-defense against any "use of force." A country could employ self-defense against any border infraction or small scale hostility. The danger in this argument is that a war could be started by a "defensive" response to a small scale use of force, such as a border infraction. However, that fear is allayed when taking into account that states are bound at all times to employ the principle of proportionality. By understanding the distinction between Article 2(4) and Article 51, it becomes clear that "a state is bound to endure acts of force that do not reach the intensity of an armed attack" (Simma et al. 1994, p. 665).

After these two approaches have been explored thoroughly, the question still remains whether a general right of self-defense exists apart from Article 51. If the right of self-defense rests in a general principle of customary law, it is a non issue that the initiating act of force is of a small scale for the right of forcible self-defense to be permitted. However, the International Court of Justice confirmed in its Nicaraguan ruling that Article 51 and customary law coincide:

> In the case of individual self-defense, the exercise of this right is subject to the State concerned having been the victim of an armed attack. Reliance on collective self-defense of course does not remove the need for this (ICJ 1986, p. 103, para. 195).

> The Court has recalled above (paragraphs 193 to 195) that for one State to use force against another, on the ground that that State has committed a wrongful act against a third State, is regarded as lawful, by way of exception, only when the wrongful act of which has not itself been the victim is not admitted when this wrongful act is not an armed attack. In the view of the Court, under international law in force today — whether customary international law or that of the United Nations system — States do not have a right of "collective" armed response to acts which do not constitute an "armed attack."(ICJ 1986, p. 110, para. 211).

It is noteworthy that when the United States illegally mined the Nicaraguan ports and armed the Contras to carry out atrocities on Nicaraguan soil, the Nicaraguan government did not resort to sending suitcase bombs to Washington, DC, and New York. Instead, the Nicaraguan government took the United States government to the

International Court of Justice where Nicaragua received a favorable ruling.

In many instances, the United States has used the alternative norm justification of self-defense to attack sovereign countries, including Grenada, Panama, Afghanistan, Sudan, Pakistan, and Yemen. The brutal sanctions and attacks on Iraq and the subsequent 2003 invasion also employed the alternative norm justification and will be discussed in chapter five.

In 1983, Ronald Reagan sent military forces to invade Grenada. The U.S. Congress was notified but not consulted. The Reagan administration dubbed the military action "Operation Urgent Fury" and purported that the reasons for the invasion were that American medical students on the island were in danger and that at the request of OECS the United States had intervened (Zinn 1999, p. 588).[18]

---

18 The Organization of Eastern Caribbean States sent a letter to the Council on 25 October 1983:

By letter dated 25 October 1983 addressed to the President of the Security Council, the representative of Saint Lucia transmitted a statement from the secretariat of the Organization of Eastern Caribbean States (OECS) stating that the OECS member countries had determined the situation in Grenada, following the assassination of the Prime Minister, several cabinet ministers and other citizens, to be a serious threat to the security of the OECS and other neighboring countries. The OECS member States were deeply concerned that the extensive military build-up in Grenada had created a situation of disproportionate military strength between Grenada and other OECS countries. Under the provisions of Article 8 of the Treaty Establishing the OECS concerning defense and security in the sub-region, member Governments had decided to take appropriate action to remove that threat. Lacking adequate military resources, the OECS had sought and received assistance from Barbados, Jamaica and the United States to form a multinational force for the purpose of undertaking a pre-emptive defensive strike in order to remove the dangerous threat to peace and security in the sub-region and "to establish a situation of normalcy" in Grenada (United Nations 2003b, para. 50).

The United States sent a letter to the Council on the same day as the letter from the OECS. The UN Repertory summarizes the American communication to the SC:

By a letter dated 25 October 1983 addressed to the President of the Security Council, the representative of the United States informed the Council

When interviewed after being rescued by American Army Rangers, American students admitted that they were surprised. On a Tuesday morning students awoke to sounds of anti-aircraft fire. Gary Ishkanian — a 24-year-old medical student on the St. George's University True Blue and Grand Anse campuses on Grenada, one of about 150 students from New Jersey among the student body of nearly 630 — awoke startled to the sound of anti-aircraft and low flying jets. "We didn't know what to think. We didn't know what was going on.... We were right there on the front line. I kept thinking to myself, 'I don't believe this is happening during midterms,'" he said (Parisi 1983, p. A35). The medical students, preoccupied with their exams, were under no military threat.

On October 27, 1983, a draft resolution was submitted that deplored the invasion of Grenada and called for an immediate halt to the intervention and a withdrawal of foreign forces from the island nation. The draft resolution failed as the result of a veto cast by the United States. The vote was 11–1 with 3 abstentions. In the aftermath of the invasion, the Reagan administration trumpeted evidence of what it claimed was a serious threat posed by Grenada, and it channeled that message through the mass media. The administration highlighted previously unknown documents that showed Grenada had signed arms deals with the Soviet Union, Cuba, and North Korea. These deals referred to arms shipments of thousands of rifles, machine guns, and grenades. The U.S. media published the most "incriminating" documents that it could find on the relationship between Grenada and Washington's adversaries. Former U.S. ambassador Sally Shelton referred to these documents as a "public relations bonanza for the U.S. government" (Crandall 2006, p. 160). The April after the invasion, the U.S. reportedly found millions of rounds of ammunition under the floor in the Cuban embassy. A few journalists questioned the administration's assertion that Grenada

---

that pursuant to the invitation of the OECS for assistance in restoring government and order in Grenada, and to facilitate the departure of the United States citizens and other foreign nationals who wished to be evacuated, the United States Government had agreed to contribute logistical, transportation and manpower support to the collective force being organized by OECS (United Nations 2003b, para. 51).

was an "armed camp," citing that some of those weapons found by the U.S. military dated back to the nineteenth century; however, these handful of voices were drowned out by the mass media's proclamations that the United States had been victorious in stopping a Cuban and Soviet take-over of Grenada.

Grenada had the right to arm itself with guns and ammunition by signing arms deals, and such actions do not warrant an invasion. However, the reported arms deals were just one effort in a public relations campaign to promote the invasion as necessary. Originally citing self-defense of American medical students studying on the island, the U.S. administration looked for any justification to persuade the American public that the invasion was necessary, even in the aftermath of the operation. The justifications, no matter how legally and logically unacceptable, were trumpeted by an obedient mass media, with hardly a dissenting voice to be heard.

Howard Zinn (1999, p. 589) cites what he calls "an unusually pointed article in the New York Times" that was published on October 29, 1983. The article, written by correspondent Bernard Gwertzman, effectively "demolishes" the American reasons for the invasion:

> The formal request that U.S. and other friendly countries provide military help was made by the Organization of Eastern Caribbean States last Sunday at the request of the United States, which wanted to show proof that it had been requested to act under terms of that group's treaty. The wording of the formal request, however, was drafted in Washington and conveyed to the Caribbean leaders by special American emissaries. Both Cuba and Grenada, when they saw that American ships were headed for Grenada, sent urgent messages promising that American students were safe and urging that an invasion not occur. . . . There is no indication that the Administration made a determined effort to evacuate the Americans peacefully. . . . Officials have acknowledged that there was no inclination to try to negotiate with the Grenadian authorities. . . . "We got there just in time," the President said. . . . A major point in the dispute is whether in fact the Americans on the island were in such danger as to warrant an invasion. No official has produced firm evidence that the

Americans were being mistreated or that they would not be able to leave if they wanted.

A high American official told Gwertzman that the true reason for the invasion of Grenada was to demonstrate that the United States was a "truly powerful nation" and had overcome the defeat of Vietnam: "What good are maneuvers and shows of force, if you never use it?" (Zinn 1999, p. 589).

Eight years after the invasion of Grenada, the *Wall Street Journal* reported that St. George, the capital of Grenada, with a population of 7500, "had 118 offshore banks, one for every 64 residents... St George's has become the Casablanca of the Caribbean, a fast growing haven for money laundering, tax evasion and assorted financial fraud" (Zinn 1999, p. 589). The case of Grenada demonstrates how a threat can be concocted or greatly exaggerated beyond proportions in order to justify the use of military force for a variety of hidden reasons. When the U.S. military invaded Grenada, it was not met by the Cuban army stationed in Grenada, but by a handful of Cuban construction workers. The United States created threats and invoked self-defense to invade Grenada to assure that it would not have political independence but that its economic policy would be decided by Washington.

Duplicating the Grenada strategy, the U.S. government shaped American public opinion both before and after the 1989 invasion of Panama through the various storylines it fed the media. During the invasion of Grenada, the American public was asked to believe that the American medical students were in grave danger and that the island was on the brink of a Cuban and Soviet take-over. During the invasion of Panama, which was dubbed "Operation Just Cause," the Reagan administration propagated the idea through the mass media that the operation was an altruistic action and that going into Panama concerned taking a stand against a drug-trafficking dictator, Manuel Noriega, who was intent on sending harmful drugs to the United States. The administration also sold the idea that Noriega supported the targeting and harassment of American citizens in Panama. This story stemmed from an American officer being killed after running a Panamanian military blockade and an American soldier being kicked and his wife reportedly threatened with rape. *Newsweek* implied that the slain officer was most likely on an intelligence mission preparing for the invasion by the U.S. military. The publication learned that "in the weeks before the invasion, officers posing as tourists visited the parts of Panama they would attack (Waller & Barry 1990).

Washington's goal was not only to capture Manuel Noriega but to eliminate the Panamanian Defense Forces and install the U.S.-friendly Guillermo Endara as president. The United States has supported autocratic and often ruthless leaders in Latin America, leaders that have accommodated American business interests, for example Pinochet in Chile and Somoza in Nicaragua. Washington had also propped up Noriega, but it withdrew support and in the second half of the 1980's began to economically punish Panama. In 1987, the United States implemented harsh sanctions against Panama and began to demonize Noriega well beyond what his criminal behavior deserved. These actions were preparing the American public for a confrontation, but the public remained largely in the dark about the actual reason for targeting Panama. In 1977, President Jimmy Carter and General Omar Torrijos, the de facto leader of Panama from 1968 to 1981, negotiated and agreed to the Panama Canal Treaties, which stipulated that all fourteen U.S. Southern Command bases located in Panama would be shut down and Panama would then effectively obtain true sovereignty in 1999 (Independent Commission of Inquiry on the U.S. Invasion of Panama 1991, p. 19). Ronald Reagan, positioning himself in 1977 for a Presidential run in 1980, opposed the treaties negotiated by Carter. As the time approached for the United States to be obligated to leave the region, the U.S. government engineered a threat to ensure long-term domination of Panama. On December 20, 1989, under George H.W. Bush, the U.S. invaded Panama.

On August 20, 1998, starting at 1:30 EST, the United States launched about 75 Tomahawk cruise missiles from warships in the Red Sea and the Arabian Sea. Washington targeted the training camps of Osama Bin Laden in Afghanistan and the Shifa Pharmaceutical factory in the Sudan, which U.S. officials accused of being a factory for the production of chemical weapons. That evening, the United States notified the United Nations Security Council by a letter that it was invoking Article 51 of the U.N. Charter to justify the strikes on Afghanistan and Sudan (Gellman & Priest 1998). President Clinton described the military strike as retaliation for the twin bombings of the U.S. embassies in Africa early in the month of August 1998. On the day of the strikes, speaking from the Massachusetts island resort of Martha's Vineyard, Clinton said, "Today we have struck back" (Gellman and Priest 1998). The United States was not under immediate threat; the strikes were acts of revenge and resulted in the bombing of a Sudanese factory that produced powdered milk, not chemical weapons.

In October 2001, following the September 11 attacks, the United States and its allies launched a military campaign against Afghanistan, which, unsurprisingly, has been wrongly regarded by many mainstream commentators as a legal and legitimate operation. This perception of legality and legitimacy of the operation has stemmed from three points: the destruction on September 11 and the deaths of 2800 civilians; the large coalition participating in the operation; and Article 51 and the implicit language of U.N. resolutions adopted after the September 11 attacks, referring to the right of collective self-defense. On October 7, 2001, the United States informed the President of the Security Council that the U.S. would, under Article 51, initiate action in Afghanistan together with other states. The U.S. stated that its action was an exercise of its inherent right of individual and collective self-defense (United Nations 2001c). The EU declared its solidarity with the United States on October 8 (United Nations 2001d). Other countries invoked Article 51 and joined the American coalition: Canada, Australia, France, the Netherlands, and New Zealand were among those to contribute to the operation in some capacity.

The United Nations condemned the "terrorist attacks" perpetrated against the United States. The United Nations did not refer to the crimes as "acts of war" but as "terrorist acts." This is important because it differentiates between an act of war initiated and waged by a country and a terrorist act carried out by an individual or group. Cases of state terrorism exist but not in the instance of September 11. Harboring terrorists is not synonymous with being a terrorist entity; otherwise, the state of Florida could easily be labeled as a terrorist state for allowing safe haven and residence to some of the worst international terrorists, including Orlando Bosch and Luis Posada Carriles, responsible for bombing a Cuban commercial airliner and other civilian targets. The September 11 attacks were attributed to Osama Bin Laden's al-Qaeda network, an organization, not a state. However, President George W. Bush, speaking shortly after the September 11 attacks said he would make "no distinction between the terrorists and those that harbor them." He likened the attacks to a declaration of war on the United States. On September 12, President Bush said in a televised statement that the attacks were "more than acts of terror. They were acts of war." The following day, he reiterated that the United States was treating the attack as an act of war, he said, "Now that war has been declared on us, we will lead the world to victory" (Beckman 2005, p. 232).

On September 12, the Security adopted unanimously Resolution 1368. The resolution condemned the attacks "in the strongest terms." The resolution made no reference to Chapter VII of the Charter and had no operative paragraphs, but it did include a preamble that reiterated the right of self-defense in accordance with the U.N. Charter. The preamble of the Resolution 1368 contained a strong message to reject terrorism a day after the devastating and shocking attacks in New York; Washington, DC; and Pennsylvania. It states, "Expresses its readiness to take all necessary steps to respond to the terrorist attacks of 11 September 2001, and to combat all forms of terrorism, in accordance with its responsibilities under the Charter of the United Nations" (United Nations 2001a). The United States justified attacking Afghanistan by citing Security Council resolutions 1368 and 1373, as well as the always convenient Article 51 of the U.N. Charter. However, no specific country was named in either resolution. Resolution 1373 reaffirmed the condemnation of the September 11 attacks. It laid out general statements on combating terrorism and referred to Chapter VII, regarding steps to block the financial resources of terrorists and to collectively police against the common threat of terrorism (United Nations 2001b).

The Security Council adopted the resolutions 1368 and 1373 to reaffirm a commitment to international cooperation in the fight against terrorism through shared policing, intelligence, border control, and the blocking of financial assets to terrorists. But to see the resolutions as a war declaration implies that the United Nations ceded a blank check to any country to invade any other country at anytime in the name of fighting terrorism. Neither resolution designated states responsible for conducting military operations, nor did they identify target states. Any legal argument that resolutions 1368 and 1373 provided United Nations authorization for the use of force is baseless and not founded on the concrete wording of the resolutions. The United States and members of its coalition invoked Article 51 of the U.N. Charter for their intervention in Afghanistan. The intervening countries were aware that they did not have an authorization to use military force in Afghanistan and thus used Article 51 as a legal argument. The legal problem for these countries is that Article 51 was not a valid justification for the intervention in Afghanistan. Article 51 pertains to responding to an immediate attack that is in progress. It does not concern a threat of attack nor does it concern retaliation for a criminal action — no matter how tragic the event. The deadliest terrorist attack on U.S. soil before September 11, 2001 was the Oklahoma City bombing in which 168 people lost their lives and over 800 were injured. For their acts of terrorism, the U.S. government prosecuted and convicted Timothy McVeigh on multiple counts of murder and Terry Nichols on manslaughter. In 2001, for the same type of crime, the U.S. bombed and invaded the sovereign country of Afghanistan. Fifteen of the nineteen September 11 hijackers, who perished in their suicide missions, originated from Saudi Arabia, but because their training camps were said to be in Afghanistan, it was targeted for collective punishment.

Before the U.S. led invasion of Afghanistan in 2001, the Taliban had achieved a nearly total ban on opium production, but after the U.S.–NATO occupied the country the ban was lifted and opium production soared — twenty-eight of thirty-two provinces "were instantly under cultivation, refining factories were reestablished; the result is that 87 percent of world trade in opium originates in Afghanistan" (Pilger 2007, p. 312). Most of the victims of the Afghan drug trade are young people in the West. Russia has lambasted the United States and NATO for refusing to eradicate the opium cultivation, and Moscow has claimed that the United States is intentionally flooding Russia with drugs. While the Afghan drug trade flourished under U.S.-NATO occupation, Washington remained busy cultivating other financial goldmines in Afghanistan. In 2010, the Pentagon announced that American geologists had uncovered a trillion dollar reserve of "untapped geological resources," including lithium, as in batteries, used for electric cars and cell phones, and "according to the *New York Times*, an internal Pentagon document said that Afghanistan could become the "Saudi Arabia of Lithium" (Fletcher 2010). While the United States oversees the lucrative Afghan drug trade and the lucrative mineral resources below the earth, it also watches over the construction of the Trans-Afghanistan Pipeline (TAP), which runs for 1,040 miles and transports natural gas from the Caspian Sea to India. After the extrajudicial killing of Osama bin Laden, who was used as a major rationale to occupy Afghanistan, the United States looks to remain for the foreseeable future in Afghanistan.

Since 2001, the United States has employed drones to carry out targeted assassinations. A person sitting in Nevada fires missiles with a joystick, much like a video game, only with deadly consequences. In December of 2009, less than a year into Barack Obama's presidency, the *New York Times* reported that "since Mr. Obama came to office, the Central Intelligence Agency has mounted more Predator drone strikes into Pakistan than during Mr. Bush's eight years in office"; the report added that the statistic is one "that the White House has not advertised" (Sanger 2009). Most of the victims of drone attacks have been women and children — what Washington labels "collateral damage." The White House claims the alternative norm of self-defense against terrorism as their legal justification for the strikes. In 2009, Harold Koh, a senior legal advisor for Obama, and former dean of Yale Law school and former director of Orville H. Schell Jr. Center for Human Rights, argued that drone strikes are legal based on self-defense and his argument was that the United States had been attacked on September 11th, nearly a decade earlier, and therefore, he claimed, firing missiles on sovereign countries with unmanned aircraft was perfectly legal (IPT News 2010).[19] Ironically Koh had been an outspoken critic of the Bush administration's counter terrorism policies. Obama has expanded on most of Bush's "terror policies" and Koh, attached to the State Department under Obama, ended up defending many of the policies that he criticized only a few years earlier.

The United States has regularly attacked Yemen with drones. In July 2011, U.S. drone attacks averaged an attack a day, resulting in considerable civilian casualties. "The Yemeni government did not allow the U.S. to conduct random attacks in the country, though it has agreed to cooperate in the fight against al-Qaeda," stated Tareq Shami, Yemen's ruling party's spokesman (Almasmari 2011). The U.S. targeted the residence of suspected al-Qaeda fighter Nader Shadadi with a drone strike, but instead killed his father, mother and, sister. A neighbor said, "Was Shadadi's mother and father [a] terrorist? They were killed by the U.S. drone. They are both over 60 years old" (Almasmari 2011). These attacks on innocent civilians have become routine. On the other hand, even when the strike hits its intended target, there is no legal justification for targeted assassinations and extrajudicial killings. President Obama, like his predecessor, has used the September 11th to attempt to create the perception of legality and legitimacy for grossly illegal actions and in the process has contributed to stretching the default rationale of self-defense to the absurd.

---

19 In Koh's first public legal justification for drone attacks in Pakistan, Afghanistan, Somalia, and Yemen, he stated: "the U.S. is in armed conflict with al-Qaeda as well as the Taliban and associated forces in response to the horrific acts of 9-11...and may use force consistent with its right to self-defense under international law...Whether a person becomes a threat depends on various considerations, including those related to the imminence of the threat, the sovereignty of the other states involved, and the willingness and ability of those states to suppress the threat the target poses" (IPT News 2010).

Cuba and the Logic of Pre-Emptive Attack

In 1962, John F. Kennedy imposed a naval blockade on Cuba to stop the Soviet Union from transferring nuclear missiles to the island nation — a blockade is considered to be a use of force. The United States defended its actions by citing self-defense. Only a year earlier, Washington had supported the failed invasion of the Bay of Pigs. The CIA had set up their largest base in the world in southern Florida, nicknamed "JM Wave," with "450 staff agents on payroll and support elements, and two thousand Cuban nationals" coordinating clandestine operations against Cuba, including the Bay of Pigs (Lynch 2000, p. 170).[20] In addition to these international acts of aggression, the United States had also attempted to assassinate Fidel Castro and situated medium range nuclear missiles in Turkey near the border of the Soviet Union, Cuba's most important ally. Considering the continuing threat from Washington, under the logic of preemptive action, Cuba would be well within its rights to attack the United States. However, this scenario is not justifiable because preemptive action has no legal backing. Article 51 of the United Nations Charter pertains to an immediate armed attack in progress and the response must be proportional and for the purpose of self-defense. Under international law, Cuba would have been within its rights to respond with an immediate and proportional force against southern Florida during the Bay of Pigs invasion; however, that was impractical because of power asymmetry.

Russia and Legitimate Self-Defense 2008

In 2002, the Bush Administration initiated a 65-million-dollar eighteen-month plan for training the Georgian military (Antelava 2004). In 2004, Mikheil Saakashvili came to power, and the U.S.

---

20 The U.S. backed Jose Mira Cardona and his United Revolutionary Front that used Miami as a base to prepare for the seizure of power after the invasion. In an effort to disguise the origins of the invasion, the CIA operated training camps in Guatemala for the Cuban-exile invasion force, painted World War II B-26 bombers to resemble Cuban planes and the disguised American military planes took off from Nicaragua to bomb Cuba. (John F. Kennedy Presidential Library & Museum 2008).

military stated that its presence in Georgia was now permanent (Antelava 2004). From 1997 to 2008, the United States sent approximately 277 million dollars in military aid to Georgia (Spiegel & Barnes 2008, p. A8). Georgia became a world leader in arms imports, increasing its military budget 30 times in the few years leading up to 2008. In April 2008, the Bush Administration pushed for Georgia to be admitted to NATO, but France and Germany opposed membership, stating Georgia was not yet ready for entry into the alliance.

In August 2008, Georgian ground and air forces attacked South Ossetia, initially killing 15 Russian peacekeepers and up to two thousand South Ossetian civilians, most of whom were holders of Russian passports. At the end of the five-day conflict, 59 Russian peacekeepers had lost their lives. The Russians responded with immediate force. The Georgian offensive was not only an attack on Russian peacekeepers but on the Russian citizens of South Ossetia. Therefore Moscow ordered tanks and troops into South Ossetia and retook the capital Tskhinvali, in what they stated was a peacemaking mission. Russia also used its air force to hit strategic targets in Georgia proper. Some Russian troops entered Georgia, for example the city of Gori, in order to create a demilitarized ring around South Ossetia, and a similar strategy was employed around Abkhazia, another breakaway region containing mostly Russian citizens. The main conflict lasted five days, and then the Russians agreed to a cease-fire and withdrew from Georgia proper, with the exception of the aforementioned demilitarized zones.

The West, in particular, the United States, criticized the Russian actions and excused Georgia from responsibility for initiating aggression against the inhabitants of South Ossetia. The Western media labeled it a Russian invasion and frequently had Georgian President Saakashvili on air for extended interviews and monologues. Despite the rhetoric against Russia, it was a clear case of Moscow responding directly to an aggression by American-backed Georgian forces, and it was clearly within its rights under Article 51 of the U.N. charter. Russia called Georgia's actions ethnic cleansing and genocide. On November 7, 2008, in the midst of the media frenzy surrounding the election of Barack Obama, the *New York Times* published a front page article describing a report released by independent military observers validating Russia's claims against Georgian aggression. The paper reported, "Newly available accounts by independent military observers of the beginning of the war between Georgia and Russia this summer call into question the longstanding Georgian assertion that it was acting defensively against separatist and Russian aggression" (Chivers & Barry 2008, p. A1). The report continued, "Instead, the accounts suggest that Georgia's inexperienced military attacked the isolated separatists capital of Tskhinvali on Aug. 7 with indiscriminate artillery and rocket fire, exposing civilians, Russian peacekeepers and unarmed monitors to harm" (Chivers & Barry 2008, p. A1). Due to Russia's strength, the U.S. response was confined to mere rhetoric. Had Russia been a militarily weak country, the deceit from Washington and its subservient media might have been a starting point for U.S. military action in support of Georgian aggression.

Chapter Four: U.S. Peacekeeping from Somalia to Haiti

Toward the end of George H.W. Bush's Presidency in 1992, American troops arrived to deliver relief supplies to suffering Somalis. The U.S. operation, authorized by Security Council Resolution 794 on December 3, 1992 and dubbed the Unified Task Force (UNITAF), remained separate from the ongoing United Nations operation in Somalia. The U.S. aimed to secure the environment and to transfer the operation to the United Nations in early 1993 for political stability and nation-building. The United States military entered Somalia and U.N. Secretary General Boutros Boutros-Ghali told the Security Council that "the first condition is that the Unified Task Force should take effective action to ensure that the heavy weapons of the factions are neutralized and brought under international control and that the irregular forces and groups are disarmed before the Unified Task Force sent on 8 December withdraws" (Boutros-Ghali 1999, p. 59). The Secretary General repeated his message to the Security Council in a letter to President Bush:

> [W]ithout this action I do not believe that it will be possible
> to establish the secure environment called for by the Security
> Council resolution or to create conditions in which the United

Nations' existing efforts to promote national reconciliation can be carried forward and the task of protecting humanitarian activities can safely be transferred to a conventional United Nations peace-keeping operation (Boutros-Ghali 1999, p. 59-60).

Despite urging by the Secretary General of the United Nations to secure the weapons and the operating zone, the Pentagon and U.S. commanders refused to disarm the Somali militia, and Bush, nearing the end of his term, did not override the military decision. The U.S. soldiers would stumble across huge weapons caches and U.S. commanders, under orders, would ignore it and leave the weapons and move on. The presence of U.S. forces over the next five months aided the delivery of food and medicine, helping to create a sharp drop in deaths from starvation and a decrease in malnourishment. During this time warlords maintained a low profile.

Boutros-Ghali said that despite the initial improvement, as a result of the military presence, the United States disregarded proper procedure to create a sustainable improvement. Boutros-Ghali (1999, p. 60) stated, "In my opinion, three critical steps were needed: disarming the warring groups; establishing a secure environment; and creating a workable division of labor between the U.S. and U.N. operations on the ground. The United States did not do any of the three."

In January 1993 Bill Clinton assumed the Presidency. The Clinton administration felt that risks and burdens could be shared between the U.S. and the U.N., and Washington appeared optimistic about working through the U.N. to pursue global policy aims — mainly as not to appear to be a unilateral policeman for the world. The Clinton administration's goal, as it had been for the Bush administration, was not to work within the U.N. but to lead the U.N., to shape its policy, and to shape the U.N. in an American mold. Despite the seamless transition of philosophy from Bush to Clinton regarding the United Nations, Republicans criticized the administration on the grounds that it was ceding U.S. sovereignty.

The Security Council, under Chapter VII of the Charter, established the follow-up operation to UNITAF, UNOSOM-II, which included a "mishmash of humanitarian, disarmament and state-building objectives throughout Somalia" (Thakur 2006, p. 56). The U.S.-led operation had entirely separate command and control from the United Nations.

> The command and control relationship between U.S. troops and UNOSCOM-II was fuzzy. In reality the U.S. troops never took operational orders from the U.N. Force Commander. Instead, the logistics unit was under the command and control of the U.S. Central Command (CENTCOM), and the civilian head of UNOSOM-II was the U.S. Admiral Jonathon Howe, appointed at Washington's request (Thakur 2006, p. 56-57).

On June 5, 1993, Somali militiamen killed twenty-four U.N. Pakistani peacekeepers and wounded another forty-four. The following day, the Security Council authorized "all necessary measures" against the perpetrator of the attacks. U.S. forces joined in the pursuit of the militants, making them more of a target for retaliation. In August, four U.S. soldiers were killed by a landmine and this event garnered the attention of the U.S. media and Congress, resulting in 400 additional U.S. troops being deployed under the command and control of CENTCOM.

By October, U.S. troops were engaged in an operation to pursue Somali warlord Mohamed Farch Aideed, and had launched a raid on his suspected hideout. The raid was conducted unilaterally, with the United Nations completely in the dark that such an operation was underway. It was not only a matter of the U.N. not approving of the mission, but that the U.N. had no knowledge of the raid (Thakur 2006, p. 57). On October 3, 1993, a battle raged and insurgents shot down two U.S. Blackhawk helicopter. When the dust settled, Somali militants had killed eighteen U.S. rangers, and wounded seventy three — one was paraded dead in the streets of Mogadishu. These deaths comprised the largest single combat casualty since Vietnam (Thakur 2006, p. 57). Mainstream media pundits and Clinton's political opponents charged his administration with ceding U.S. authority, command, and control to the United Nations. The administration remained silent about CENTCOM having complete command and control over the operation, and mute about the U.S. having pursued a unilateral agenda separate from the U.N. mission. Instead, the Clinton Administration let the blame fall squarely on the U.N. for what the media and right wing opponents were describing as an incompetent organization incapable of carrying out such an operation.

The U.S. peacekeeping operation caved in almost immediately as President Clinton ordered a full withdrawal of U.S. troops from Somalia within six months. At UNITAF's peak, 37,000 U.S. soldiers were in Somalia (Rawski & Miller 2004, p. 367). While the U.S. troops were being withdrawn from Somalia, White House legal advisors were drafting Presidential Decision Directive (PRD) 25, which laid out conditions for future involvement:

> PRD 25 placed strict conditions on future U.S. involvement in U.N. operations, including a policy review to determine whether U.S. participation served a legitimate foreign policy interest, a pledge to consult Congress before voting in favor of the creation or expansion of a peacekeeping force in the Council, and a prohibition on the placement of U.S. troops under U.N. command (Rawski & Miller 2004, p. 362).

U.S. resistance to the establishment and expansion of U.N. peacekeeping operations directly resulted in the failure of the international community to intervene and prevent the genocide of nearly a million Rwandan civilians from April to July 1994. On April 21, 1994, after "intense lobbying by the U.S. State Department," the Security Council passed Resolution 912, which recalled most of the U.N. peacekeeping force in Rwanda, the U.N. Assistance Mission in Rwanda (UNAMIR) (Rawski & Miller 2004, p. 362). As genocide was underway — hundreds of thousands of innocent men, women, and children enduring torture and being massacred in Rwanda — the State Department instructed the U.N. Ambassador to aggressively oppose any effort at this time to preserve a UNAMIR presence in Rwanda'" (Rawski & Miller 2004, p. 362).

It is hard to find a more blatant example of governmental hypocrisy than the American, British, and French imposed no-fly zones in Iraq, which were implemented two years earlier in 1992, and Western involvement in Bosnia, with these same countries showing a complete indifference to the genocide in Rwanda. While the American, British, and French air forces illegally patrolled Iraqi skies and bombed targets, ostensibly in the name of human rights, information was passed to the U.S., French, and Belgium governments that warranted urgent and serious attention. On January 12, 1994, General Romeo Dallaire, a Canadian military commander of the United Nations Assistance Mission in Rwanda (UNAMIR), informed the U.N. Department of Peace-keeping (DPKO) that an informant knew of plans for mass killings of Tutsis by Hutu forces who were also stockpiling weapons. He requested the authorization to seize the stockpiles but was denied by the DPKO because Security Council authorization was needed. Dallaire informed the Ambassadors of the United States, Belgium, and France about the report (Boutros-Ghali 1999, p. 130). These governments received information that the situation was extremely severe months before the massacres and, out of lack of interest, chose not to act. The weapon of choice to massacre the Tutsis was the machete, and a modest U.N. peacekeeping presence could have prevented the Rwandan genocide. Instead, the Hutus slaughtered over eight hundred thousand Tutsis and committed widespread rape and torture. The international community failed to respond. The United States and its Western allies did nothing to stop the massacres, yet in less bloody conflicts with achievable political solutions, these countries worked to create the perception that military intervention in the name of humanitarianism was an absolute necessity.

Haiti

In 1991 the Haitian people chose Jean-Bertrand Aristide as their first democratically elected President. Aristide's victory surprised Washington, which had been confident that Marc Bazin, a World Bank Official and their preferred candidate, would easily win; he received only 14 percent of the vote (Chomsky 2000, p. 145). The response from the United States "was to shift aid to anti-Aristide elements . . . and to honor asylum claims for the first time." (Chomsky 2000, p. 14). In September 1991, seven months after taking office, rebels overthrew Haiti's first elected government and forced Aristide into exile. The Organization of American States and the

United States reacted by announcing an embargo on Haiti, but the U.S. routinely violated the embargo and allowed for exceptions on a "case by case" basis (Schaeffer-Duffy 2005, p. 6). The George H.W. Bush administration exempted U.S. firms from the embargo, while simultaneously proclaiming the government of Haiti to be illegal. Subsequently, Bill Clinton expanded on the same policy and U.S. trade to Haiti nearly doubled. The administration maintained its connection with the regime in Port au Prince, but did its best to conceal the details. According to Human Rights Watch, the Clinton administration refused to release 160,000 pages of documents that likely contain "embarrassing revelations" on Washington's dealings with the illegal and brutal regime (Chomsky, 2000, p. 146). Chomsky (2000, p. 146) writes on U.S. companies circumventing the embargo:

> Officials of the U.S. Justice Department revealed that the Bush and Clinton Administration had rendered the embargo virtually meaningless by authorizing illegal shipments of oil to the military junta and its wealthy supporters, informing Texaco Oil Company that it would not be penalized for violating the presidential directive of October 1991 banning such shipments. The information, prominently released the day before U.S. troops landed to restore "democracy" in 1994, has yet to reach the general public, and is an unlikely candidate for the historical record.

Due to intense international pressure and an influx in unwanted refugees attempting to reach U.S. shores, Aristide was reinstated in 1994, and Washington required that he adopt their neo-liberal economic agenda. In 1996, the Haitian people elected Rene Garcia Preval and in 2001, despite an electoral boycott, reelected Aristide to the presidency. By 2004, rebel groups were carrying out acts of violence in the city streets. Aristide appealed for international help, but the U.S. Secretary of State said there was "no enthusiasm" in the United States or Caribbean countries to step into the conflict (*CNN.com* 18 Feb. 2004). On February 24, Aristide was removed from office, forced into exile by U.S. military personnel that surrounded his house and the presidential palace in the early hours of the morning and forcibly put him on a plane and transported him for twenty hours to an unknown destination, which turned out to be the Central African Republic. Washington maintained that he resigned of his own free will. "The long-simmering crisis is largely of Mr. Aristide's making," the White House stated. "His failure to adhere to democratic principles has contributed to the deep polarization and violent unrest that we are witnessing in Haiti today" (Sanger & Schmitt 2004, p. 1.1). Ira Kurzban served as General Counsel for the Haitian government for thirteen years (1991-2004). On February 25, he stated, "I believe that this is a group that is armed by, trained by, and employed the intelligent services of the United States" (Goodman and Scahill 2004). Democratic Senator John Kerry, while campaigning for the U.S. presidency, said of the Bush administration, "They hate Artistide." Kerry pledged that as President he would consider an attempt to persuade the rebels from trying to overthrow Aristide by deploying a peacekeeping force and gave a message to the rebels: "You're not going to take over. You're not kicking him out. This democracy is going to be sustained. We're willing to put in a new government, [a] new prime minister, we're willing to work with you, but you're not going to succeed in your goal of exile [of President Aristide]" (Halbfinger 2004, p. A20).

The United States, France, and Canada deployed troops to Haiti to calm the situation, and they labeled the contingent the "Multinational Interim Force" (MIF), of which the U.S., as usual, maintained command. Aristide flew to Jamaica and then to South Africa, but was barred from returning to Haiti. The United States introduced U.N. Resolution 1529 on February 29 on behalf of the "Friends of Haiti Group," which included Brazil, Canada, Chile, France, and the United States. France was the first country to call for the resignation of Aristide. A year earlier, Aristide had demanded France pay over $21 billion in restitution for the crimes it committed during the many years of colonial rule in Haiti, thus Aristide's departure couldn't have come soon enough for Paris. On April 30, the Council unanimously passed the resolution establishing the U.N. stabilization Mission in Haiti (MINUSTAH), which was authorized for an initial period of six months with the possibility of renewal. It was also requested that the authority of the MIF be transferred to MINUSTAH. On November 29th, the Security Council extended the mandate of MINUSTAH to July 2005 with the intention to further renew the mandate at that time (Bureau of International Organization Affairs 2005, pp. 36-37).

In 2004, Bush won reelection. Therefore, John Kerry's commitment to reinstate the democratically elected Aristide as president of Haiti could not come to fruition. Instead, the United States, France, and Canada solidified a coup d'état by transferring the authority of a unilateral force supporting an illegal action to a multilateral legitimate peacekeeping force sanctioned by the United Nations. Democratic Congressman Charles B. Rangel of New York expressed that the Bush administration had collaborated and assisted the rebels, whether gunmen or politicians, in "a coup d'état." He said, "We're on the side of the crooks and the thieves, and you're asking me how do we distinguish among them" (Marquis 2004, p. A8). Aristide remained exiled in South Africa until March 17, 2011, when he returned to his homeland, greeted by throngs of supporters.

CHAPTER FIVE: IRAQ

*"All Members shall settle their international disputes
by peaceful means in such a manner that international peace and
security, and justice, are not endangered." — Article 2 (3) of the
U.N. Charter*

*"Try to reach an agreement or compromise by discussion
with others." — Definition of negotiate, the New Oxford–American Dictionary*

During the Iran–Iraq war (1980 to 1988) the United States
supported Saddam Hussein and covertly sent arms to Iran. Henry
Kissinger stated the U.S. policy bluntly when he said at the beginning of the war, "I hope they kill each other." In 1990, the Kuwaiti
government drove down oil prices at a time when Iraq was in need
of funds, antagonizing Saddam Hussein. He accused Kuwait of si-
phoning off Iraqi oil reserves by slant drilling across the border. On
July 25, 1990, Saddam met with April Glaspie, the U.S. Ambassador
to Iraq, and expressed to her a need for higher oil prices. Glaspie
responded, "I know you need funds. We understand that and our
opinion is that you should have the opportunity to rebuild your
country. But we have no opinion on the Arab–Arab conflicts, like
your border disagreement with Kuwait. . . . James Baker has direct-

ed our official spokesman to emphasize this instruction" (Hoagland 1990, p. A15). These instructions closely mirrored positions taken at that time by Washington as State Department officials had "publicly disavowed any American security commitments to Kuwait" (Hoagland 1990, p. A15). Considering Washington's indifferent response, Iraq promptly invaded Kuwait on August 2nd, violating the U.N. Charter and international law.

After Saddam attacked Kuwait, polls showed that American support for intervention remained split. The issue divided Congress as well. The United States had a ready and willing ally in Britain, but all other European countries, as well Arab members of the U.S. ad hoc coalition, required that the U.S. obtain a Security Council resolution under Article 42 of the U.N. Charter in order for them to contribute militarily (Apple 1990, p. A1). Bush Administration officials contended that the U.S. could use force against Iraq under Article 51 of the U.N. Charter. Opposition remained in the Congress. Bush remarked, "History is replete with examples where the President had to take action" without authorization from the U.S. Congress, and he added for emphasis that he would "have no hesitancy to do so" (Lewis 1990, p. A18). The protracted buildup of U.S. troops in the Gulf region showed the situation was neither to be an imminent or urgent threat and, therefore, it was legally obligatory to receive Congressional authorization.[21]

Fifteen years earlier, in 1975, Morocco had invaded Western Sahara. The dynamics were nearly identical to the Iraq–Kuwait situation: an "autocratic Arab country invading a small, resource-rich Arab country" (Zunes 2001). Morocco expelled most of the Western Saharans into desert exile, resulting in a humanitarian catastrophe. Indonesia invaded East Timor the same year and massacred more than 200,000 people — one-third of East Timor's population. A year earlier, in 1974, Turkey had expelled the Greek majority from Cyprus, and the island remains divided until today. Turkey con-

---

21 In 1973, the Congress enacted the War Powers Act that required the President to notify the Congress within 48 hours of deploying troops where "imminent involvement of hostilities is clearly indicated," and the Act states that troops must be withdrawn unless the Congress authorizes the military operation (Lewis 1990, p. A18).

tinues to occupy the northern third of Cyprus and has killed more than 2,000 civilians, including some Americans. The most glaring example of occupation and annexation is Israel's stranglehold and suffocation of Palestinian territories, with Israel brazenly violating numerous U.N. resolutions. In the three years preceding Iraq's invasion of Kuwait, Israel killed "more than 1,000 Palestinians, including scores of children, hundreds of homes were demolished, orchards and other crops were uprooted, and scores of activists were forced into exile. All of these were illegal under international law" (Zunes 2001). Every one of these actions was supported by military and economic aid from the United States, and in some cases Washington continues its ongoing support. However, Iraq's incursion into Kuwait was met with a different response from Washington, which felt a sudden need to uphold international law. On November 13, 1990, at a joint press conference in Canada, Secretary of State James Baker said, "The economic lifeline of the industrial world runs from the Gulf, and we cannot permit a dictator such as this to sit astride the economic lifeline" (Baker 1995, p. 336). Baker said the average American should understand he was talking about their "jobs," later adding that although he meant what he said, perhaps he should have said their "economic prosperity."

Enforcing Council resolutions through sanctions or military force falls under Chapter VII of the Charter. The Charter's predisposition is to favor solutions by peaceful means and to avoid or limit violence. Chapter VI Article 33 states that all peaceful avenues need to be exhausted.[22] Immediate collective force should only be authorized when no diplomatic solution is possible and to halt widespread atrocities, such as the 1994 genocide in Rwanda. If enforcement action would cause a worsening of violent conflict, negotiations should be continued in order to find a peaceful, diplo-

---

22 Under Chapter VI, *Pacific Settlement of Disputes*, of the UN Charter, Article 33(1) states, "Parties to any dispute, the continuance of which is likely to endanger the maintenance of international peace and security, shall, first of all, seek a solution by negotiation, enquiring mediation, conciliation, arbitration, judicial settlement, resort to regional agencies of arrangements, or other peaceful means of their own choice."

matic solution. The purpose of the U.N. Charter is to limit violence as much as possible and to promote positive diplomacy.

In the last days of August 1991, State Department spokesperson Margaret D. Tutwiler declared that Saddam Hussein's request for a debate with President George H.W. Bush and Prime Minister Thatcher was "sick, and it doesn't deserve a response" (Apple 1990, p. A1). By August 29th, the United States had expelled thirty-six Iraqi diplomatic personnel. The Soviet Union was cooperating with the United States on most aspects of the Iraqi situation, but it criticized the expulsions, warning that such actions could cause "a spiral of escalation" (Apple 1990, p. A.1).

In early September, an unverified report surfaced that Iraqi soldiers in Kuwait were emptying babies from incubators and leaving them on the floor to die. No pictures, video, or interviews of grieving mothers surfaced. A month later a 15-year-old girl testified before the Human Rights Caucus of the United States Congress. Referred to only as "Nayirah," because she was said to fear reprisals by the Iraqis, she choked back tears and said she had witnessed babies being dumped from incubators. For the next five weeks President Bush reiterated the story to exhibit the monstrosity of Saddam Hussein, and seven U.S. Senators specifically referred to "Nayirah" and the incubator babies in the Senate debate on approving military action. The final margin of the vote authorizing military action was five votes (Knightly 2001). John MacArthur (2004, p. 54) writes, "Of all the accusations made against the dictator [Saddam Hussein], none had more impact on American public opinion than the one about Iraqi soldiers removing 312 babies from their incubators and leaving them to die on the cold hospital floors of Kuwait City." After the war ended, it came to light that "Nayirah" was the daughter of the Kuwaiti Ambassador to the United States, and Hill and Knowlton, the largest PR firm in the world, had arranged for her to "testify" before Congress and coached her in acting. The accusations of Iraqi soldiers taking babies from incubators were completely false:

> [At the Human Rights Congress] Hill & Knowlton and Congressman Lantos had failed to reveal that Nayirah was a member

of the Kuwaiti royal family. Her father, in fact, was Saud Na-sir al-Sabah, Kuwait's Ambassador to the U.S., who sat listen-ing in the hearing room during her testimony. The Caucus also failed to reveal that H&K vice-president Lauri Fitz-Pegado had coached Nayirah in what even the Kuwaitis' own investigators later confirmed was false testimony...Human rights investiga-tors attempted to confirm Nayirah's story and could find no witnesses or other evidence to support it...When journalists for the Canadian Broadcasting Corporation asked Nasir al-Sabah for permission to question Nayirah about the story, the ambas-sador angrily refused (Stauber & Rampton 1995, pp. 173-174).

The group "Citizens for a free Kuwait," which was financed by the Kuwaiti government in exile, had inked a $10 million contract with Hill and Knowlton to create the perception of legitimacy for the use of force against Iraq (Knightly 2001). The U.S. obtained U.N. Security Council authorization to expel Iraq from Kuwait, which, in addition to Nayirah's acting, helped to secure enough votes in Congress, which passed in the House of Representatives 250 to 183 and in the Senate 52 to 47.

The United States has routinely attempted to use the Security Council as a legitimating instrument. Policies that appear explicitly controversial and unacceptable are sometimes brought to the Unit-ed Nations in order to launder them into "legitimate" courses of action (Snidal & Abbott 1998, p. 18-19). Legitimation by the Secu-rity Council not only lessens criticism against an action, but third-party states are more likely to participate in burden sharing. The 1991 Persian Gulf War is an example of burden sharing: 36 coun-tries participated in the war. Although the United States contrib-uted the most human and financial resources, the coalition partners made significant contributions, especially when compared to the meager offerings made by third party states during the 2003 uni-lateral invasion of Iraq. A Security Council mandate provides gov-ernments tangible benefits, most notably decreased financial costs and greater third-party commitment of military personnel, which most importantly translates into augmented domestic support — as it bolsters the public's confidence that their government is tak-ing forcible action for proper reasons (Voeten 2001, pp. 847-848).

James Baker acknowledged that the principle reasons for obtaining a U.N. Security Council authorization for the First Gulf War were to increase domestic support and to influence the U.S. Congress, which had been relatively uncooperative toward any plans to use unilateral force without a Security Council mandate (Baker 1995, p. 278).[23]George H.W. Bush would later say, "Without the United

23 In poll after poll, domestic support registers significantly higher for UN sanctioned interventions than for those that are unilateral. A 2007 Gallup poll revealed that 70 percent of Americans felt that a foreign policy goal of "building democracy in other nations" was important while 31 percent thought it was very important (Sanders 2007, p. 39). However, 68 percent of Americans, polled in a PIPA/Chicago Council poll, felt that working through the United Nations would be more successful because "such efforts will be seen as more legitimate" (Sanders 2007, p. 39). Public opinion polls have also demonstrated that the American public generally supports the United Nations and desires its government to work within the UN (Russert 1994; Rawski & Miller 2004). Because of this aspiration, governments have pressure to adhere to international obligations and legislators feel a constraint to authorize the use of force only when taken through the Security Council. In 1950, 83 percent of the American public approved of the concept of the United States supplying soldiers to the United Nations in case a similar situation to the Korean War arose (Chapman & Reiter 2004, p. 889). In July 1964, there was 58 percent approval (as opposed to 19 percent disapproval) for a UN army in Vietnam and Southwest Asia. In 1967, 60 percent of the population was in favor of a UN solution to the Vietnam War, while 32 percent were opposed. In a 1995 poll, 60 percent of the American public said that they preferred to stay out of a conflict or let another country take the lead if "a dictator was pursuing aggression against another country" and the UN refused to take the lead (Chapman & Reiter 2004, p. 889). Other polls, including ones relating to the First Gulf War, the former Yugoslavia, and the situation on the Korean peninsula, showed similar numbers. World public opinion towards the U.N. is generally just as, or more positive than American public's attitude of the organization. From October 2005 to January 2006, the international polling firm GlobeScan in conjunction with the Program on International Policy Attitudes (PIPA) of the University of Maryland polled 37,572 people in 32 countries for the BBC World Service. The results were that the UN was seen as "mainly positive" by 59 percent of the respondents as opposed to 16 percent that viewed the UN as "mainly negative." This was a drop of ten percent from the 2004 poll, but still a large majority. The view that the United Nations was "mainly positive" was spread across all continents and held by people in countries across the spectrum, including rich and poor, democratic

Nations [I might have] sent a considerable force to help" (Meisler 1995, p. 272). On August 7th, five days after Iraqi soldiers entered Kuwait, President George H.W. Bush authorized the deployment of 150,000 American soldiers to the Gulf region (Wells 2005, p. 86).

On February 22, the *Wall Street Journal* reported, "Iraq agreed to withdraw its forces from Kuwait if the United States and its allies accept a cease-fire in the Persian Gulf conflict and agreed to halt economic sanction" (Seib 1991, p. A1). The Soviet Union tabled a plan to avoid a ground war, but the United States was unwilling to negotiate. The Bush Administration rejected the proposal outright and declared that the war would continue. Military officials stated that the bombing of Iraq would intensify during negotiations. The bombing campaign intensified but negotiations were non-existent. On February 24th, the United States and Britain said that the Security Council had all but exhausted its efforts to promote a peaceful solution (Lewis 1991, p. A1). The U.N. Secretary General Javier Perez de Cuellar said in a statement to the Council, "Openings toward a cessation of the conflict have been clearly revealed in the past two days. The United Nations — and, if I may add, its Secretary General — are passing through a most trying and in some respects painful

---

and autocratic, and large and small countries. Europeans and Asians had responses that were "especially positive." Germany had 80 percent of respondents that viewed the UN as "mainly positive" as opposed to just 6 percent saying "mainly negative." Indonesia also had an 80 percent positive response, Afghanistan a 79 percent positive response, South Korea a 76 percent positive response, and Nigeria a 75 percent positive response, to name just a few examples. The permanent five member states all had a majority of respondents view the UN as "mainly positive." The United States had 52 percent positive to 36 percent negative, France 52 percent positive to 33 percent negative, Great Britain 66 percent to 24 percent negative, and Russia 38 percent positive to 14 percent negative. China was not included in the poll (World Public Opinion.org 2006). Iraq was the only country polled in which the majority of the respondents had a "mainly negative" view of the U.N. with 40 percent negative and 34 percent positive, which reflects outrage over the U.S.-British war and occupation against Iraq and the deadly decade-long sanctions that killed over a million Iraqis (World Public Opinion.org 2006).

experience" (Lewis 1991, p. A19). On the evening of February 24, 1991, the United States launched the ground war.

Two days after the ground war began, the Soviet Union and Iraq requested that the United Nations declare a truce. The Soviet Union stated that Saddam Hussein had ordered his troops to withdraw from Kuwait, as demanded by the Security Council. Despite Iraqi troop withdrawal from Kuwait being the central focus of the crisis, the United States and Britain rejected the request for a truce and claimed that Saddam Hussein must abide by all U.N. resolutions. India called for a truce, stating that a truce would permit Iraq to withdraw its forces to safety. Baghdad Radio announced that the withdrawal of troops was ordered, "in accordance with United Nations Resolution 660" (Lewis 1991, A12).

The United States rejected any call for a cease-fire and intensified their attacks on retreating Iraqi soldiers. The U.S. Defense Intelligence Agency estimated the Iraqi military deaths to be between 50,000 and 150,000 (Meisler 1995, p. 272). The U.S. ground assault extended deep into Iraqi territory despite the mandate of Resolution 678 referring only to Iraqi withdrawal from Kuwait. While Iraqi soldiers were retreating to comply with U.N. Resolution 660, the United States massacred them wholesale in the desert. The U.S. Air Force bombed the first and last vehicles and created a gigantic traffic jam column. Fighter jets then proceeded to attack the entire column, in which thousands were reported to have died (CBC 2 Mar. 1991).

> Allied planes bombarded the retreating Iraqis. The bombing left one long Iraqi column of more than a thousand [some estimates say closer to two thousand] burned-out cars, trucks, tanks, and other vehicles with the bodies of two hundred to three hundred Iraqis lying nearby. American television and newspapers ran fearful images of the devastation and dubbed the scene "the highway of death." (Meisler 1995, p. 271).

It is no secret that Iraq possesses the world's second largest oil reserves after Saudi Arabia. Energy expert Paul Roberts, author of *The End of Oil*, writes, "The first Gulf War was the first military conflict in world history that was motivated entirely about oil. Interest in oil had not only prompted Saddam to invade but had largely defined the world's reaction" (Roberts 2004, p. 105). In the run up to the war, protesters marched in cities across the world and chanted the slogan "No blood for oil!" At the same time, government spokesmen depicted the suffering of Kuwaiti people, while diplomats spoke candidly in private about the threat to their national oil interests.

> While government spokesmen made much of Kuwaiti suffering, behind closed doors, diplomats were focused almost entirely on the loss of Kuwaiti oil and, more to the point, whether the attendant price spike would tip the world into recession. Indeed, Washington's first decisive act was to obtain assurances from Riyadh that Saudi Arabia would pump enough extra oil to cover the loss of combined Kuwaiti and Iraqi production, thus preventing what everyone agreed would be the worst aspect of Saddam's aggression — a long term disruption of oil supply (Roberts 2004, p. 105-106).

The United States and Britain used the symbolic power of the United Nations to garner domestic and third country support to remove obstacles to an expanded agenda, one that reached well beyond the Council's mandate. Furthermore, the United States and Britain, which would have gone to war unilaterally, violated the Charter by refusing to negotiate a peaceful settlement and rejecting a valid proposal to avert a ground war. The case of the First Gulf War not only demonstrates the power and legitimacy of the U.N. Security Council but the tragic consequences when states co-opt that power to create the perception of legitimacy for aggression. Most of the public heard the original Council mandate in general terms and failed to see the blatant disregard for the actual contents of the mandate by Washington and its allies.

No Fly Zones in Iraq

The United Nations Charter should be understood within its intended context, which is to minimize violence. U.N. resolutions are not to be interpreted broadly to garner support for the use of maximum force, but narrowly as to minimize force, if it is necessary at all. Resolution 678 (1990) authorized force to remove Iraqi forces from Kuwait, and the statement on "restoring international peace and security" must not be viewed outside the context of that mission. The resolution did not authorize the overthrow the Iraqi government, the enforcement of weapons inspections, or the imposition of no-fly zones. U.S. and British officials claimed that Saddam Hussein breached the negotiated cease-fire and, therefore, under resolution 678, they had legal authorization to use punitive force against Iraq. However, a simple reading of the Charter refutes such a notion. Article 2(4) prohibits the use of non-defensive force, and Security Council authorization is required to use force once a permanent cease-fire has been negotiated. Lobel and Ratner (1999, p. 129) write, "Armed responses to breaches of cease-fire agreements cannot be made by individual states; a new Security Council authorization must be adopted."

The United States zeroed in on the phrase "restoring international peace and security" in resolution 678, using it to justify no-fly zones in northern and southern Iraq. Washington also invoked Resolution 688, which condemned the Iraqi government for repression of the Kurds in the north and demanded a change in policy and access for humanitarian organizations (United Nations 1991a). But resolution 688 contains no mention of foreign troops on Iraqi soil or no-fly zones, and because no authorization was granted the Chinese and Russians expressed disapproval for any foreign military presence on or over Iraqi territory without the permission of the Iraqi government.

In Chapter VII of the U.N. Charter, Article 42 states that if coercive measures fail the Council may enforce adopted resolutions by taking "such action by air, sea, or land forces as may be necessary to 'maintain or restore' international peace and security." However, resolution 678 is restricted in that it states only to "*restore* international peace and security." No possible reading of Resolution 678 can be interpreted as a legal argument for a maintenance force subsequent to the permanent cease-fire in February 1991. Iraq permitted 500 armed U.N. guards to protect humanitarian workers, but the U.S., Britain, and France unilaterally created no-fly zones, citing resolutions 678 and 688 as legal authority, and regularly bombed

Iraq. In August 1992, the proposed southern no-fly zones were widely criticized in the United Nations. Opponents of the zones said that the proposal "went beyond any legal mandate and the Non-Aligned Movement said that any move to attack Iraqi planes would not receive Security Council backing" (Lobel & Ratner 1999, p. 133). The United States, Britain, and France patrolled the northern and southern zones until France withdrew from the northern zones in 1996 and from the southern zones following the heavy four-day bombing campaign of Operation Desert Fox — December 16-19, 1998. The United States and Britain imposed the no-fly zones until their invasion of Iraq in 2003.

Five years before George W. Bush and Tony Blair launched "shock and awe" on a false pretext, Bill Clinton attempted a craftier deception. In January and February of 1998, United States officials, including President Bill Clinton, threatened the use of force against Iraq if it did not provide unconditional access to international weapons inspectors. Then-Secretary of State Madeline Albright warned the Iraqi government that the military campaign would not involve "pinpricks" but "substantial strikes" (U.S. Department of State 1998). In late February, the U.N. Secretary General Kofi Annan visited Baghdad, but Albright threatened to ignore the work of the Secretary General, declaring, "We [the United States] will pursue our national interest" if Annan returns with an agreement unsatisfactory to the United States (Morgan 1998, p. A15). On February 23, while in Iraq, Annan secured a memorandum of understanding, signed by himself and the Deputy Prime Minister of Iraq, in which the Iraqi government agreed to open eight "presidential sites" to international inspectors (Crossette 1998 p. A8). On March 2, 1998, the Security Council unanimously endorsed the memorandum of understanding in Resolution 1154 (United Nations 1998a). Not a single country asserted that Resolution 1154 provided authorization for unilateral force and a majority of the countries stated that force could only be authorized through an additional resolution. Following the meeting, U.S. Ambassador to the U.N., Bill Richardson, said the vote was a "green light" for President Clinton to attack Iraq if he felt that Iraq was not in compliance with allowing unconditional access for the inspectors (Lobel & Ratner 1999, p. 124).

In late February 1998, Scott Ritter, a top U.N. weapons inspector, met with Richard Butler, the appointed Chairman of the United Nations Special Commission (UNSCOM).[24] According to Ritter, Butler made a chart with two timetables and told Ritter they needed "an accelerated inspection timetable." He labeled one timetable "inspections" and the other one "military action" and wrote on the side of the board the dates from March 1 to March 15. Butler drew a ring around March 8 on the chart and said to Ritter, "We need to have a crisis with Iraq by this date," tapped the board, and continued "so that the U.S. can complete its bombing campaign by this date", and he circled March 15 (Ritter 2005, pp. 271-272). "I have been told that the U.S. has a bombing campaign prepared which needs to be completed in time for the Muslim religious holiday that begins on 15 March," said Butler. Ritter (2005, p. 272) writes, "I sat there, stunned. What I was observing was nothing less than total collusion between a United Nations Official, Richard Butler, and the USA over military action that had not been sanctioned by the Security Council."

Ritter developed a strategic list of sites for weapons inspections in Iraq, designed to progress from known sites of interest to highly sensitive locations. UNSCOM's Deputy Chairman Charles Duelfer, a former U.S. State Department official, told Ritter that his proposal needed to be simplified, that it contained "too many legalities" (Ritter 2005, p. 270). Instead, Duelfer wanted to add the Iraqi Ministry of Defense (MoD) to the list, even though he and many other high ranking U.S. officials knew that no substantive reason existed to inspect it. The Clinton administration uniformly and wholeheartedly supported the proposal to demand inspection of Iraq's MoD. Ritter said to Duelfer of the proposed inspection, "But we have no WMD-related reason to inspect [the MoD]." Duelfer responded, "Tariq Aziz gave us the reason when he told Butler that to try and inspect the Ministry of Defense meant war. We cannot allow the Iraqis

---

24 Richard Butler would later be scolded by Kofi Annan for using undiplomatic language.

to pick and choose which site we can and cannot inspect. This is about process, not substance" (Ritter 2005, p. 270). The Clinton administration raised the bar and made the test of Iraqi cooperation a full inspection of their Ministry of Defense, and Washington, understanding that Iraq was unable to open the Ministry and that it contained no proscribed materials, warned Iraq that to avoid a military attack they must allow its full inspection.

The United States prepared a significant strike against Iraq: "All American forces in the Persian Gulf went on high alert and initial strike elements actually launched and went into orbit" Ritter told reporters (Lederer 2001). However, the Iraqi government yielded to Washington's threats and opened the MoD for inspections, surprising the Clinton administration. On March 11, Kofi Annan said that inspectors were "able to go into a site they never have been able to go to: the Ministry of Defense...They had five days of inspections without a hitch" (*Reuters* 11 March 1998). Ritter (2005, p. 277) writes that, much to the consternation of American officials, UNSCOM inspectors reported nothing prohibited in the MoD:

> In the end, nothing proscribed was found at the Ministry of Defense. Madeleine Albright, in France, was furious when the French told her that according to their sources, Iraq and UNSCOM were getting along famously, and the inspectors were actually finished with the inspection. The American military had been placed on high alert, and everyone in the U.S. chain of command was confident that there would be a window for military action against Iraq.

The Clinton Administration employed a typical U.S. or U.S.-led NATO conflict negotiation tactic: the United States and its allies raise the bar too high and demand a concession they know their adversary is unable to deliver. The ultimatum is usually not necessary to achieve a diplomatic and peaceful solution, and the media ignore the unreasonable ultimatum and instead focus on other parts of the proposal, which are not adopted, but only because they are accompanied by the unreasonable demand. When the adversary cannot agree to such a demand, the U.S. officials and their allies label the adversarial government intransigent and exclaim that "all diplomatic avenues have been exhausted." In March 1998, the Iraqi government met the unreasonable ultimatum of the United States and allowed UNSCOM to inspect their MoD, *temporarily* thwarting a military strike.

The United Nations reassigned Scott Ritter to Bahrain, and Charles Duelfer led the next UNSCOM inspection team in Iraq. Under Duelfer, and with his full support, the CIA put "structural engineers on the team, who evaluated each one of Saddam's palaces from the standpoint of a potential aerial attack" (Ritter 2005, p. 277). Ritter (2005, p. 277) writes that Duelfer was involved in "perpetrating a sham, turning UNSCOM into little more than an espionage tool to be used by the CIA to spy on Saddam Hussein." In addition to an abundance of accusations of UNSCOM being used for espionage activities, Washington manipulated UNSCOM to provide justification for the maintenance of genocidal sanctions. According to Ritter, in August 1998, a U.S. Counselor at the U.S. Mission in New York told him that the United States was not the least interested in "real disarmament" but "just the illusion of disarmament" and "UNSCOM's job was to do only that which legitimize the continuation of economic sanctions." After seven years of service, Scott Ritter resigned as weapon inspector.

Richard Butler, an Australian diplomat had been appointed Chairman of UNSCOM in 1997. In late October 1998, Baghdad accused UNSCOM officials of providing intelligence to Washington and, therefore, would terminate the remaining inspections. The Iraqi government stated that inspections could not go forth with Richard Butler as the head of UNSCOM, and that sanctions must be lifted. Despite this rhetoric, inspectors continued their work in Iraq. Richard Butler (2000) argues that it is doubtful that American intelligent services would find information collected by UNSCOM valuable, considering the advanced technology at the disposal of the CIA. Nevertheless he admits that it is a possibility that information was passed from UNSCOM to U.S. intelligence agencies:

> "Is it possible that some UNSCOM data, without my knowledge made it into the vast U.S. hopper of information used in U.S. military targeting? Maybe. Perhaps, some U.S. nationals on our staff received telephone calls from military planners in

Washington: 'We're interested in bombing such and such a laboratory in Baghdad....Such conversations aren't inconceivable" (Butler 2000, pp. 198-199).

The 2003 Iraq invasion displayed inefficiency in U.S. intelligence, crushing the mythology of the omnipresent CIA. It is not only conceivable but probable that the Pentagon and U.S. intelligence agencies regarded information from UNSCOM inspectors as highly valuable.

In mid-November 1998, Washington's Ambassador to the United Nations called Butler to suggest that his staff evacuate Iraq (Butler 2000, p. 202). Butler (2000, p. 218) writes that UNSCOM carried out inspections as late as the week of December 3-9 before they yielded to the American suggestion to evacuate. The Clinton administration launched Operation Desert Fox on December 16th, and repeatedly justified the military strike by accusing Iraq of expelling the UNSCOM inspectors. In 70 hours of intensive bombing, according to Pentagon officials, the United States and Britain launched 415 cruise missiles, and fired an undisclosed number of laser guided bombs and "other ordinance" (Robinson 1998, p. A01).[25]

President Boris Yeltsin denounced the U.S. and British actions, saying, "by taking unprovoked military action, the United States and Britain have crudely violated the U.N. Charter and generally accepted principles of international law and the norms and rules of responsible behavior by states" (Lippman & Drozdiak 1998, p. A55). The Russians recalled their Ambassador from Washington to show their outrage over the unilateral strikes. Madeline Albright said that the Russians were trying to "shoot the messenger" when "the problem was Saddam Hussein" (Lippman & Drozdiak 1998, p. A55). The lower house of the Russian Parliament apparently dis-

---

25 The European Union and NATO countries, Japan, South Korea, Australia, and New Zealand supported the strikes. Italy and France expressed reservations. Italy called for an immediate halt to the strikes and stated a change was needed for an international strategy based on economic sanctions that were "painful and ineffective." France stated that it deplored military action but that Saddam Hussein was to blame and bore the responsibility for the situation (Lippman & Drozdiak 1998, p. A55).

agreed with her assessment and passed a resolution stating that the United States and Britain had engaged in "barbarous acts" and accused the two nations of "international terrorism" (Lippman & Drozdiak 1998, p. A55).

The Chinese echoed the Russian sentiment. Chinese Foreign Minister, Sun Yuxi, urged the United States to bring an immediate halt to military action in Iraq and stated, "The United States has not received permission from the U.N. Security Council, and took unilateral action in using force against Iraq, violating the U.N. Charter and international principles" (Lippman & Drozdiak 1998, p. A55). China's Ambassador to the United Nations said, "We were deeply shocked by this act and we condemn it. This unprovoked military action is completely groundless" (Lippman & Drozdiak 1998, p. A55).

Lobel and Ratner (1999, p. 125) write, "The refusal of the United States to accept limitations on its power by the Security Council thus depended on creatively interpreting the Council's resolutions to accord authority, despite contrary positions of a majority of its members." U.S. officials such as Undersecretary of State and former UN Ambassador Thomas Pickering cited Resolution 1154 and argued that it did not preclude the unilateral use of force. Pickering argued that he was able to persuade members not to include language that explicitly required the U.S. to return to the Council for authorization (Lobel & Ratner 1999, p. 125). The U.S. and Britain would have vetoed a resolution that prohibited force without additional authorization; the best resolution the Security Council could adopt was one which did not mention the use of force. Authorization for force must be stated in a resolution. The prohibition is a part of the U.N. Charter and the use of collective force is the exception to that prohibition, to be carried out in extraordinary circumstances. The manipulative and twisted logic of U.S. officials attempted to turn that on its head, and in essence, claimed that force is authorized by the Council unless a resolution prohibiting a military attack is passed.

Sanctions and the Reverse Veto

In August 1990, with the passage of Resolution 661, the Security Council imposed comprehensive sanctions on Iraq, prohibiting all importation or exportation of goods outside the sanction system, including oil. The United States, with British support, ensured that the sanctions committee maintained a vast list of proscribed goods, from water purification systems to shoelaces. An independent UNICEF (United Nations Children's Fund) report lists categories of imports that were prohibited: "medicines, food imports, agricultural inputs — fertilizer, pesticides, spare parts, Industrial/Commercial, inputs/parts, other spare parts, fuel, educational materials, water purification/supply inputs" (Shah 2005). John Pilger details some of the everyday items that Washington and London made certain never reached the Iraqi people:

> "Iraq is prohibited from importing fertilizer and animal feed equipment. This has caused the collapse of much of the nation's agricultural production. Baby food and enriched powdered milk are banned, forcing mothers who are too malnourished to breast-feed to give their babies sugared water or sugared black tea. Most of these children have died; they are known as the "sugar babies.""...In the hospitals, people are being operated on without anesthetic because vital equipment is blockaded, along with stethoscopes, X-ray equipment, scanners, water purifiers, bandages, sutures and medical swabs. A consignment of ambulances from France was stopped. Customs officers at London's Heathrow Airport recently confiscated antibiotics from a humanitarian delegation flying to Iraq and threatened to prosecute. Children's clothes, sanitary napkins, light bulbs, schoolbooks, paper, pencils, shoelaces-all are banned or have been lost in a cynical delaying process" (Pilger 1998).

Joy Gordon (2002) spent three years researching the Iraq sanctions regime:

> "Over the last three years, through research and interviews with diplomats, U.N. staff, scholars, and journalists, I have acquired many of the key confidential U.N. documents concerning the administration of Iraq sanctions. I obtained the documents on the condition that my sources remain anonymous. What they show is that the United States has fought aggressively through-

out the last decade to purposefully minimize the humanitarian goods that enter the country. And it has done so in the face of enormous human suffering, including massive increases in child mortality and widespread epidemics. It has sometimes given a reason for its refusal to approve humanitarian goods, sometimes given no reason at all, and sometimes changed its reason three or four times, in each instance causing a delay of months."

The U.S. routinely called for holds on specific parts that rendered entire machines or systems inoperable and used its veto to create an extensive list of prohibited "dual use" items. Proscribed items extended to all facets of Iraqi life, including basic medical services. In 2001, the United States "placed holds on $280 million in medical supplies, including vaccines to treat infant hepatitis, tetanus, and diphtheria, as well as incubators and cardiac equipment" (Gordon 2002).The blocking of basic medical supplies, food, and humanitarian items to Iraq constituted a more than decades long violation of international humanitarian and human rights law, including serious breaches of the Geneva Conventions and the Convention on the Rights of the Child. The sanctions were illegal under the Geneva Protocols as they targeted the civilian population (violations of Articles 48 and 51(2)); indiscriminately attacked the population, using sanctions as a means for collective punishment (violating Article 51(3); and used starvation as a method of warfare (violating Article 54). The refusal to permit adequate humanitarian assistance passage to Iraq also breached Art. 3 common to the 1949 Geneva Conventions, Art. 18 (2) of Additional Protocol II, Article 23 of the Fourth Geneva Convention, and Article 70 of the Additional Protocol I. Under international law no exceptions are permitted to the free passage of humanitarian aid. Additionally, there is a good case to be made, based on the structure of the policy and its results, that the sanctions breached the Convention on Genocide, the rules of distinction, Article 6.1 of the International Covenant on Civil and Political Rights, as well as the principle of proportionality. Russia, France, and China made efforts to lift or reform the sanctions but were blocked by the U.S. and Britain through the use of the reverse veto, which kept the sanctions policy active due to the absence of a stated time limit in Resolution 661.

In June 1991, Pentagon officials admitted that Iraq's electrical grid had been targeted by air strikes to break the civilian economy. One planning officer said, "People say, 'You didn't recognize that it was going to have an effect on water and sewage.' Well, what were we trying to do with sanctions — help out the Iraqi people? No. What we were trying to do with the attacks on infrastructure was to accelerate the effect of the sanctions" (Gellman 1991, p. Al). The results, Gordon (2002) reports, "were widespread outbreaks of cholera and typhoid — diseases that had been largely eradicated in Iraq — as well as massive increases in child and infant dysentery, and skyrocketing infant and child mortality rates." The aerial bombardment and the sanctions obliterated the water and sewage systems and by 1996 every sewage system was inoperable. Prior to the First Gulf War, the vast majority of Iraqis had access to potable water (95 percent in cities and 75 percent in rural areas). In February 2000, the Associated Press reported that "most of the disputed contracts" were "for equipment to improve Iraq's dilapidated oil industry, power grid, and water sanitation infrastructure" (Winfield 2000).

The 661 Committee conducted its business in private, no doubt wary of the outcry from the international community. By 1995 an estimated one million Iraqis had died as a direct result of sanctions, of which 500,000 were children under the age of five. In May 1996, Lesley Stahl of 60 Minutes interviewed then-U.N. Ambassador Madeline Albright: "We have heard that a half a million children have died [referring to the sanctions]. I mean, that's more children than died in Hiroshima. And, you know, is the price worth it?" Stahl asked. Albright infamously replied, "...we think the price is worth it" (Mahajan 2001). In 1996, the Security Council implemented the Oil for Food program (a proposal that had been rejected by Iraq in 1990), but it did little to ease the suffering of the population. Philippe Heffinck, UNICEF Representative in Baghdad affirmed, '... there is no sign of any improvement since Security Council Resolution 986/1111 [oil-for-food] came into force" (UNICEF 1997). The goods that arrived from oil revenue amounted to approximately "$175 per person a year, or less than 49 cents a day" (von Sponeck

2002, p. A15). Iraqi diplomats pointed out that this was far less than the $400 dollars a year the U.N. spends on imported food for their de-mining dogs (Gordon 2002). A November 1997 UNICEF (1997) report stated, "The most alarming results are those on malnutrition, with 32 per cent of children under the age of five, some 960,000 children, chronically malnourished — a rise of 72 per cent since 1991. Almost one quarter (around 23 per cent) are underweight — twice as high as the levels found in neighboring Jordan or Turkey." The same month President Clinton declared, "The sanctions will be there until the end of time, or as long as he [Hussein] lasts" (Crossette 1997).

The U.S. and British governments pushed the sanctions policy and held it in place, but the genocidal effects weighed on the minds and hearts of officials in the U.N. Secretariat. In autumn 1998, the Assistant U.N. Secretary General and U.N. Humanitarian Coordinator for Iraq, Denis J. Halliday, resigned in protest. "I am resigning [as Assistant Secretary General of the United Nations], he wrote, "because the policy of economic sanctions is totally bankrupt. We are in the process of destroying an entire society. It is as simple and terrifying as that... Five thousand children are dying each month... I don't want to administer a programme that results in figures like these." In February 2000, Hans von Sponeck, who replaced Halliday, also resigned. "This current [sanctions] policy is not just at fault, it is criminal," he stated (von Sponeck 2001). Days later, Jutta Burghart, the head of the World Food Program, announced her resignation, forcefully criticizing the sanctions. That week, a group of seventy U.S. congressmen, Democrats and Republicans, called the sanctions "infanticide masquerading as policy" (BBC News 2000). After extensive debate and objections by Washington and London, the sanctions committee permitted a UNICEF official, Anupama Rao Singh, to issue a report before the committee. On March 20, 2000, she delivered her report on the critical humanitarian situation in Iraq; it included the following: "25 percent of children in the south and central governorates suffered from chronic malnutrition, which was often irreversible, 9 percent from acute malnutrition,

and child-mortality rates had more than doubled since the imposition of sanctions" (Gordon 2002).

The following year the United States proposed "smart sanctions", which were little more than a public relations effort amidst a
storm of international criticism. "'Smart sanctions' only reaffirm the
position of Iraqi women and children as bargaining tools in the continuing dispute between Washington and Baghdad," von Sponeck
stated. "It serves to distract from the critical disarmament issues at
hand" (von Sponeck 2002). In June 2002, the Economist predicted
that Iraq's GDP would decline under smart sanctions. Tun Myat,
von Sponeck's replacement as U.N. coordinator in Iraq noted, "'No
matter how much you modify the U.N. humanitarian program it is
not designed for — and it will never be — a substitute for normal
economic activity. . . . The markets are quite full of things; the problem is whether or not there are people who have the purchasing
power to buy them" (von Sponeck 2002). France and China agreed
to the proposal and, as a result, Washington released some holds on
contracts with French and Chinese companies ($80 million in Chi-
nese contracts). However, Russia vetoed the proposal and Washington placed nearly every Iraqi contract with a Russian company
on the hold list. "Smart sanctions" became the Goods Review List
(GRL), and, in May 2002, the Council passed the new program and
Washington immediately removed holds on $740 million of Rus-
sian contracts. The role of reviewing the $5 billion dollars worth of
holds transferred to UNMOVIC (United Nations Monitoring, Verification, and Inspection Commission) and the IAEA (International
Atomic Energy Agency), both of which found few items deserving of being on the GRL or that "warranted the security concern
that the United States had originally claimed" (Gordon 2002). The
sanctions committee released hundreds of holds with little effect as
Washington and London not only blocked implementation of relief
measures but sabotaged the Oil for Food program by concocting a
system of "retroactive pricing" and withholding their Council votes
to set a price for Iraqi oil until after a buying period had passed. By
waiting until after the buying period to set a price, buyers naturally became discouraged, unwilling to buy oil for which they had

no idea what the price would be at time of purchase. By late 2002, Iraqi oil revenues had fallen by 40 percent from the previous year. Additionally, the new sanctions program still involved a vast list of items classified as "dual use" and Washington and London used this to continue suffocating the Iraqi population, while refusing to acknowledge Iraq's steady disarmament.

In 2005, Amy Goodman interviewed Democratic Governor Bill Richardson, who served as U.N. Ambassador during the second Clinton administration, and asked him the same question put to Madeline Albright nearly a decade earlier:

> Goodman: ...the sanctions led to the deaths of more than a half a million children, not to mention more than a million Iraqis...Do you think the price was worth it, 500,000 children dead?

> Richardson: Well, I stand behind the sanctions. I believe that they successfully contained Saddam Hussein. I believe that the sanctions were an instrument of our policy... Well, I believe our policy was correct, yes (Democracy Now 2005).

Washington sought to create a perception that Saddam Hussein bore the responsibility for the humanitarian crisis in Iraq and charged that he had illegally used oil revenue to purchase weapons, inflating the figures, without evidence, to "billions of dollars"; however, it was American companies, with support from Washington politicians, which committed the biggest sanctions violations. In 2005, a Senate investigative committee presented "documentary evidence" that the Bush administration knew of "illegal oil sales and kickbacks paid to the Saddam Hussein regime but did nothing to stop them"; the oil shipments involved "dwarfed" previous "allegations by the Senate committee against individual U.N. staff and European politicians" (Borger & Wilson).

The sanctions were lifted, not with relief for Iraqis but with the mass destruction and death of the 2003 U.S. and British invasion. Since then, the Security Council has passed only sanctions with time limits, which require re-passage upon expiration, thus eliminating the highly problematic reverse veto. Washington continues to violate the will of the international community with its unilateral sanctions against Iran and an illegal fifty year embargo on

Cuba. In 2010, the U.N. General Assembly voted for the 19th straight year to condemn the U.S. embargo on Cuba. The vote was 187 to 2 with the United States and Israel casting negative votes. Three U.S. protectorates abstained: Marshall Islands, Palau, and Micronesia. Had the reverse veto not been in effect with Resolution 661 and had the sanctions been allowed to expire after Iraq's withdrawal from Kuwait, Washington would likely have attempted, with London, to unilaterally suffocate the Iraqi economy. Instead, the United States and the United Kingdom handcuffed the Security Council, for over a decade, to a sanctions regime that violated international law and the spirit of the United Nations and capitalized on the U.N. brand to create the perception of legitimacy for a policy that killed over a million innocent Iraqis, most of them children.

2003 Invasion

In October 2002 President Bush declared, "America must not ignore the threat gathering against us. Facing clear evidence of peril, we cannot wait for the final proof — the smoking gun — that could come in the form of a mushroom cloud" (*White House Press Office* 7 Oct. 2002). Washington infamously accused Iraq of having stockpiles of biological, chemical, and nuclear weapons.

In October 2002 the Democrats in Congress, with a few exceptions, handed George W. Bush a blank check authorizing force against Iraq.[26] Leading up to the March invasion, Washington and

---

26 A Newsweek poll, conducted in the United States in January of 2003, a few months before the U.S. invasion of Iraq, found that 31 percent of the American population supported a unilateral U.S. attack and 65 percent opposed an attack. However, support for U.S. military action against Iraq if the U.S. "joined together with its major allies, with the full support of the United Nations Security Council" registered at 85 percent with only 15 percent still opposing the use of force (Pew Research Center 2003). The reality of U.N. legitimacy has led the United States to attempt to launder aggressive force through the United Nations. Some members of Congress, Hilary Clinton being one notable person, who voted in October 2002 to give George W. Bush the authority to use force in Iraq, later gave the ridiculous excuse that it was not an authorization to use unilateral force, but an action to give President Bush more authority to work at the Security Council. It appears that this

London referred to the threat posed by the alleged Iraqi weapons of mass destruction as "imminent." Weapons inspectors found no sign that Iraq possessed WMD. The Russian, Chinese, French, and the majority of the other non-permanent Council members remained unconvinced Iraq was a threat, especially considering the U.S.-British no-fly restrictions imposed on Iraq and the unilateral bombings carried out against the country. From March 2000 to June 2003, Hans Blix headed the United Nations Monitoring, Verification and Inspection Commission (UNMOVIC), which monitored Iraqi compliance with international obligations. Blix said, "It was very hard to see that the Iraqis were terribly dangerous in the year 2002 or 2003 (Flach Film 2004). Iraq claimed it had no weapons and that it could not prove a negative, and, in 2005, after Iraq had been bombed to rubble, the White House acknowledged Iraq did not possess WMD.

The mainstream American media pushed the 2003 invasion to such an extent that if a tribunal were held to prosecute those responsible for the illegal attack, media executives would deserve to be tried alongside government and military officials. A report issued by Fairness and Accuracy in Reporting (FAIR) on 18 March 2003 concluded that network newscasts, in their pre-invasion coverage were " dominated by current and former U.S. officials" and "largely exclude[d] Americans who are skeptical of or opposed to an invasion of Iraq." The study found that "76 percent of all sources were current or former officials leaving little room for independent or grassroots views. Similarly, 75 percent of U.S. sources (199/267) were current or former officials" (*Fairness and Accuracy in Reporting* 18 Mar. 2003).[27] It also found that a large discrepancy existed between the viewpoints of on-air sources and public opinion:

---

reasoning shows a lack of responsibility for giving President Bush authority to use force; however, the rationale, although weak, still demonstrates the desire of members of Congress to be perceived as working within the constraints of the Security Council.

27 The two week study (spanning 30 January to 12 February 2003) examined on-camera network news sources quoted on Iraq and found what amounted to the media acting in large part as an extension of government public relations. The study examined 393 on-camera sources.

At a time when 61 percent of U.S. respondents were telling poll-sters that more time was needed for diplomacy and inspections (2/6/03), only 6 percent of U.S. sources on the four networks were skeptics regarding the need for war. . . . Sources affiliated with anti-war activism were nearly non-existent. On the four networks combined, just three of 393 sources were identified as being affiliated with anti-war activism — less than 1 percent. Just one of 267 U.S. sources was affiliated with anti-war activism — less than half a percent (*Fairness and Accuracy in Reporting* 18 Mar. 2003).

Another FAIR study found that during the war 64 percent of all U.S. network sources "were pro-war" while "71 percent of U.S. guests favored the war" (Broughel & Rendell 2003). Of the 10 per-cent of sources that were anti-war, only 3 percent were U.S. sourc-es, and 6 percent were non-Iraqi sources. The report state: "[V]iew-ers were more than six times as likely to see a pro-war source as one who was anti-war; with U.S. guests alone, the ratio increases to 25 to 1" (Broughel & Rendell 2003).[28] A 2003 study used seven differ-ent polls from January through September of 2003 and found the public's belief in misinformation correlated directly to its approv-al for the war. The study, conducted by the Program on Interna-tional Policy (PIPA) at the University of Maryland and Knowledge Networks, found that "before and after the Iraq war a majority of Americans have had significant misperceptions and these are highly related to support for the war in Iraq" (*World Public Opinion* 2003). The study's data show a direct link between the information the media disseminate to the public, the public's misperceptions, and the public's support for the war:

> An in-depth analysis of a series of polls conducted June through September found 48 percent incorrectly believed that evidence of links between Iraq and al-Qaeda have been found, 22 percent that weapons of mass destruction have been found in Iraq, and 25 percent that the world public opinion favored the U.S. going

---

28 This report examined 1,617 on-camera sources for three consecutive weeks starting the day after the bombing began. The sources appeared in stories about Iraq on the nightly newscasts of six news channels and television networks.

to war with Iraq. Overall 60 percent had at least one of these misperceptions. (*World Public Opinion* 2003).[29]

---

29 The study found that of the people with none of the three misperceptions, only 23 percent supported the war. The percentage jumped to 53 percent in support of the war for those that held one of the misperceptions, 78 percent for those with two of the misperceptions, and 86 percent for those that held all three misperceptions. The study concluded that the variations of misperceptions based on the source people received their news from "cannot simply be explained as a result of differences in the demographics of each audience, because these variations can also be found when comparing the rate of misperceptions with demographic subgroups of each audience" (*World Public Opinion* 2003). A percentage of the American public believed, and some still do, that Iraq was directly involved in the attacks of September 11, 2001, despite U.S. and other foreign intelligence agencies asserting that those claims are completely without foundation. Before the U.S.–British invasion of Iraq in 2003, 20 percent believed that Iraq was directly involved in the September 11 attacks, and 13 percent stated that they had witnessed conclusive evidence that linked Iraq directly to the attacks. The study's June through September 2003 polling, which asked people to respond conclusively, showed the percentage of people believing in the direct Iraq-September 11 connection staying at 20-25 percent while 33-36 percent thought that "Iraq gave al-Qaeda substantial support." However, an August 2003 *Washington Post* poll asked people if it was "somewhat likely" that Saddam Hussein was involved himself in the September 11 attacks, and 69 percent answered in the affirmative. These misperceptions translated into an increase in support for the war and people's incorrect belief that the war was legitimate.

Before the war began, Americans held misperceptions that were conclusively linked to their approval for going to war. In February 2003, a month before the invasion, the PIPA study showed that of the Americans that believed Iraq was directly involved in the September 11 attacks, 58 percent supported President George W. Bush to use unilateral force against Iraq and to bypass the United Nations. The percentage fell to 37 percent approval for individuals who believed Iraq gave support to al-Qaeda but was not involved in September 11 attacks. The percentage dropped another 5 percent to 32 percent for those who believed there was only a little contact between al-Qaeda members and Iraqi officials. Of the people who believed there was no contact between Iraq and al-Qaeda, the approval for the war fell to 25 percent. Some might think that these misperceptions are a result of people's failure to pay attention to the news; however, the PIPA study found that people who "pay greater attention are more likely to have misperceptions." The exception to this finding is people whose news source is print media because the more they pay attention, the fewer misperceptions they acquire.

Funding for media outlets comes largely from ad revenue and, therefore, networks wrap themselves in the flag in the manner of a slick political candidate or salesman. Today's American mass media networks are subsidiaries of a handful of major corporate conglomerates that have financial interests in the defense and military industrial complex which profits from military conflict or receives revenue from political candidates that run ads during election season. In 2004, President Bush, Senator John Kerry, their political parties and allied groups spent more than $600 million on advertising (MPR 2004).

In 2008, CNN correspondent Jessica Yellin, a reporter for MSNBC during the run up to the 2003 Iraq invasion, told CNN's Anderson Cooper in an interview, "The press corps was under enormous pressure from corporate executives to make sure the war was presented 'in a way that was consistent with the patriotic fervor in the nation and the president's high approval ratings'" (Bauder 2008). Yellin said that the higher the President's approval ratings went, "the more pressure she felt from the news executives" to do positive stories on Bush; she indicated to Cooper that her bosses would reject critical stories of Bush and in their place air only positive ones (Bauder 2008). Other journalists were fired or taken off assignments for speaking critically of the pending war in Iraq. Phil Donohue was one of the only critical voices in the mainstream media that challenged the Bush Administration's reasoning for invading Iraq. Despite having the highest rated show on the network, MSNBC fired Donohue in February 2003, just before the invasion. "Well, we were the only antiwar voice that had a show, and that, I think, made them very nervous. I mean, from the top down, they

---

Another factor is the relationship between political positions and misperceptions. Political positions did correlate with misperceptions, but the study found that these misperceptions were not a result of bias. "The level of misperceptions varies according to Americans' political positions. Supporters of President Bush and Republicans are more likely to have misperceptions. However, misperceptions do not appear to only be the result of bias, because a significant number of people who do not have such political positions also have misperceptions" (World Public Opinion 2003).

were just terrified," Donohue said. "We had to have two conserva-tives on for every liberal. I was counted as two liberals. [W]e were very — I was isolated, and we were very alone at the end. And then we had nobody supporting us, and our numbers were very decent" (*Media Matters for America* 29 Oct. 2004).

During wartime, democratic rulers use the rationale of "sup-porting the troops" and "rallying around the flag" to push through measures that otherwise would not be considered acceptable to the public. Margaret Thatcher, British Prime Minister from 1979 to 1990, had an approval rating of 25 percent after three years in office, but, in 1982, she saw that approval rating jump to 59 percent after Britain reinvaded the Falklands (Klein 2007, p. 138). She used her new surge in popularity, acquired from the British public's pride in reasserting one of its last colonial dominions, to use force against "the enemy within." She authorized the use of state force to crush the unions: eight thousand baton-swinging police attacked a plant picket line, resulting in over seven hundred injuries. The number of injuries soared into the thousands during the course of the strike (Klein, 2007, pp. 137-138). Thatcher unleashed the most expansive internal undercover intelligence campaign in British history aimed at destroying the powerful miners union. The president of the min-ers union, Arthur Scargill, said, "[It] was the most ambitious coun-ter-surveillance operation ever mounted in Britain" (Klein 2007, p. 138). These policies were directly linked to Thatcher's appeal to crush "the enemy within" after they had defeated the "external en-emy" in the Falklands.

Once a ruler takes a country to war, the mandate is often ex-tended, and new policies in unrelated areas are proposed, common-ly referred to as "mission creep." The British public overwhelmingly opposed the 2003 Iraq invasion before it was launched, but after it began, the numbers reversed and the British public overwhelm-ingly supported the war, because their soldiers were in harm's way. For moral theorists or moral human beings, there is little sense in this type of thinking. However, rulers use this sentiment among the masses to push additional policies and to extend the initial strategy of the operation.

By the time America elected Barack Obama in 2008, more than a million Iraqi people had perished and four million had become refugees. Meanwhile, in 2005, Washington had begun construction, in Baghdad, on the largest embassy in the world, measuring one hundred and four acres-- almost eighty football fields and about the size of Vatican City.

Within a deprived Iraqi society, this ostentatious compound has all the amenities of an upscale retirement community: office buildings, homes, stores, restaurants, gymnasium, movie theatre, tennis courts, swimming pool, and an American club. The embassy construction cost U.S. taxpayers over a billion dollars, and the annual maintenance costs approach two billion dollars. While Americans luxuriate at the landscaped, Olympic sized pool, Iraqis suffer from impure drinking water and the effects of insufficient and unreliable electrical power. Rather than fulfill his campaign promise of exiting Iraq, President Obama retained the previous administration's defense secretary — Robert Gates, and re-branded the brutal occupation. Obama attempted to retain roughly 15,000 troops in Iraq, but the Iraqi government refused to grant complete immunity for U.S. military personnel. Therefore, Obama was forced to follow the agreement that George W. Bush had signed with the Iraqi government, requiring the removal of combat troops by the end of 2011. This fact did not stop Obama from disingenuously trumpeting that he had ended the war. While U.S. combat troops left Iraq, U.S. mercenaries stayed behind and a small American city within Iraq is left situated on the banks of the Tigris. This embassy remains a constant reminder to Iraqis of the hand that brought mass destruction, suffering, and tragedy.

CHAPTER SIX: DESTROYING YUGOSLAVIA

Yugoslavia broke with the Soviet Union in 1949 and thus be-came a strategic buffer for the United States and the West against the Soviet block. Yugoslavians had a good standard of living; the country remained open to trade and the International Monetary Fund (IMF), its citizens enjoyed free movement, and it welcomed foreigners. Yugoslavia was socialist, politically decentralized, and maintained extensive economic liberalization.

In the winter of 1949, the Economic and Central Council of the Yugoslav Trade Unions called for the establishment of 215 coun-cils, and after a few months, over 500 economic organizations had worker councils (Lakicevic 1969, p. 60).[30] In June 1950, The Federal Assembly passed the first law addressing worker's self-manage-ment. The Basic Law described workers' self-management:

> Factories, mines, carriers, transport, trade, agricultural, forest, public utility, and other state economic enterprises, as the gen-eral people's property, shall be managed by working collectives on behalf of the social community within the framework of the state economic plan. . . . The working collectives shall exercise

---

30 These instructions were published in a document entitled "Instructions on the Establishment and Functioning of Workers Councils in State Controlled Economic Enterprises."

this right of management through workers councils (Singleton 1976, p. 126).

Over the next few years, the practice of worker management extended to numerous other sectors of life and government. These included public health, education, culture, and social insurance. The governmental administration organs that directed these services were exchanged for entities of self-government (Lakicevic 1969, p. 60). In 1952, 8,800 enterprises were under worker self-management, and 4,187 enterprises were comprised of fewer than thirty workers; the average workforce consisted of 114 employees (Singleton 1976, p. 132). Workers, usually unskilled laborers, went on strike when they sought those improvements in conditions, most commonly they appealed for higher wages or demonstrated against management's failure to live up to the rules of self-management. From 1958 to 1978, workers went on strike 3,000 times, and nearly seventy-five percent of all participants were unskilled laborers (Library of Congress Federal Research Division 1992, p. 82). Protests were not directed toward the worker managed councils but towards government bodies and the heads of enterprise:

> Strikers directed their discontent not at worker's councils, nominally in control of the workplace, but at enterprise directors, local government bodies, and executive organs—those perceived as making the decisions most responsible for worker's discontent (Library of Congress Federal Research Division 1992, p. 82).

The Yugoslav Government was "pragmatic" with strikers and "officials viewed strikes as an indication of inadequate implementation of self-management" (Library of Congress Federal Research Division 1992, p. 82). Workers were free to organize to improve the conditions of their employment, and the government responded constructively.

Deemed a land of minorities, no group within Yugoslavia possessed more than a regional majority, and many Yugoslavians lived in small ethnic communities not located within their corresponding nations. The cities, and the majority of the towns, were ethnically mixed. Treaties decided the borders of Yugoslavia's six republics, based on ethnic and cultural factors, in 1944, 1947, 1953, and 1956. Only Serbia and Montenegro had previously been recognized as states in 1878.

In census reports, many identified themselves as Yugoslavs, especially idealistic party members and army officers, to express their belief in the Yugoslav idea and socialism. Others identified with where they lived or grew up and not with their ethnic background. Before 1963, the census failed to recognize the political identity of Muslims. In the 1971 census, many Muslims changed their identity choice from Yugoslav to Muslim. Bosnia was not a constituent nation or a nationality, and was not listed on the census. Had Muslims in Bosnian territories been given the option to mark Bosnian, many would have checked that box (Woodward 1995, p. 36). For many others, deciding what to put on the census was a difficult choice because they were from a mixed background. Nevertheless, the decision to identity oneself with a national identity was completely voluntary — citizens had a right not to choose. Selecting national identities was used for the census and for other official documents, but it also served to protect culture, to give ethnic communities language rights, and to provide psychological security. In addition, Belgrade gathered national identity figures to be used for the national quota system, referred to as the national key, which ensured proportional representation for appointments in the military, the equal distribution of resources and investments, representation for cultural activities, and appointments to public offices. The quota system guaranteed proportional representation in the rotation of the federal prime minister (Woodward 1995, pp. 36-37). Federal policy unified the country. Susan Woodward, author of *Balkan Tragedy*, elaborates on Belgrade's policy:

> "[Federal policy was] a complex balancing act in the international arena and a mixed economy and political system that provided governmental protections of social and economic equality and of shared sovereignty among its many nations...Far from being repressed, national identity and rights were institutionalized by the federal system, which granted near statehood to the republics, and the multiple rights of national self-determination for individuals" (Woodward 1995, pp. 21-22, 45).

Often regurgitated in the West, especially in the United States, is the notion that Tito's charisma or dominance of the communist party was responsible for dropping an iron lid on historical, ethnic, or religious tensions in Yugoslavia. This simplistic view derives from a knee-jerk anti-communist outlook, as if to say the ingredients for civil war were there all along but were temporarily smothered by an overarching power. This is a misguided analysis. Good public policy created a fair economy and ensured the equality under the law of all Yugoslavians. Tito, an ethnic Croatian, made policy that created a balance among the Yugoslav nations. This historical fact is often suppressed in the United States in favor of a convenient mythology that one man or a politburo held down the flames of civil war for decades.

Since 1949, Yugoslavia had "regularly negotiated loans from the International Monetary Fund (IMF) and implemented marketizing and decentralizing economic reforms to satisfy IMF conditions" (Woodward, 1995, p. 1). From 1979 to 1989, Yugoslavia suffered a decade of austerity and became increasingly reliant on IMF loans. Despite uncertainty the country remained open and multicultural and maintained a relatively prosperous way of life (Woodward 1995, pp. 36-37). In 1984, [U.S.] National Security Decision Directive NSDD 133, entitled "United States policy towards Yugoslavia labeled Secret Sensitive," made destabilizing Socialist Yugoslavia official policy. Washington declassified a censored version in 1990, similar to NSDD 54 from 1982, which stated that the strategic goal was to work to create Western market economies including "expanded efforts to promote a 'quiet revolution' to overthrow Communist governments and parties." In 1990 the International Monetary Fund (IMF) seized control of Yugoslavia's central bank, which "resulted in a diversion of state revenues away from the usual transfer of payments to the republics and into the payments on Yugoslav's external debt with the IMF's Paris and London clubs" (Ljubisic 2004, p. 70). Davorka Ljubisic, born in Zagreb, Croatia, writes that the shock therapy architects proceeded to "massively privatize the public sector leading to massive bankruptcy and liquidation of socially owned businesses and the banking system — the core of Yugoslavia's noble and successful experiment in market social-ism with its unique form of socialist (workers') self-management. This massive privatization led to massive unemployment, a result of massive layoff of redundant workers" (Ljubisic 2004, p.70). By breaking the country economically, the United States and Euro-pean allies played a classic game of divide and conquer, aimed at demolishing what they viewed as a bad example of decentralized socialism and worker empowerment. A professor emeritus of Eco-nomics at the University of Ottawa, Michel Chossudovsky (1996, p. 37), writes, "While local leaders and Western interests shared the spoils of the former Yugoslav economy, they have entrenched socio-ethnic divisions in the very structure of partition. This permanent fragmentation of Yugoslavia along ethnic lines thwarts a united re-sistance of Yugoslavs of all ethnic origins against the recolonization of their homeland."

In March 1989, Ante Markovic, a Croatian businessman and a reformist calling for Yugoslavia to become a Western "free-market democracy," became Prime Minister. President Bush, Secretary of State James Baker, and National Security Advisor Brent Scow-croft met with Markovic in the Oval Office and encouraged him to continue with economic reforms (*Associated Press* 13 October 1989).[31] Markovic informed them that these changes would result in a twenty percent increase in unemployment and were "bound to bring social problems," increased political tension, and increased ethnic tension among the country's republics and autonomous re-gions (*New York Times* 14 October 1989, p. 4).

The West's central motivation for supporting Yugoslavian uni-ty came from the international banking community desiring repay-ment of debt.[32] In January 1990, Yugoslavia initiated an economic

---

31 Markovic asked the Bush Administration for financial assistance and help with Yugoslavia's 19-billion-dollar national debt. He sought to at-tract American foreign investment and joint ventures, telling American officials that legislation had been passed to allow for such moves (*New York Times* 14 October 1989, p. 4).

32 Markovic met with bankers in New York, including Treasury Secretary Nicholas Brady, U.S. Federal Reserve Board chairman Alan Greenspan, World Bank president Barber Conable, and the IMF managing director

"stabilization" plan under a World Bank Structural Adjustment Loan (SAL II) and an IMF Stand-by Arrangement (SBA) and Markovic asked Western powers to delay collection on Yugoslavia's debt — a temporary postponement not a cancellation. The West — the Bush Administration, the European Union, and the IMF — all refused the slightest rescheduling of the debt repayment (Sachs 2005, p. 127). Forced to make cuts for debt repayment, the Yugoslav federal government suspended payments to the republics and the two autonomous provinces, helping to instigate the process of separatism and secessionism. The suspension of payments to the republics resulted in de facto secession. Actors became more reliant on local and republican support than federal support. Belgrade was hamstrung with debt servicing. From January to June 1990, real wages dropped by 41 percent, and by the end of the year, inflation had risen to more than 70 percent (Chossudovsky 1997, p. 246).

The CIA leaked a document in November 1990 that predicted Yugoslavia would violently disintegrate within a year and a half. It stated that the "Yugoslav experiment" in market socialism had failed (Bennett 1995, p. 173). On November 5, 1990, the U.S. Congress passed the 1991 Foreign Appropriations Bill. Section 184, which specifically dealt with Yugoslavia and took effect six months after passage on May 5, 1991. It cut all funding to Yugoslavia and instructed the U.S. Secretary of the Treasury to use the "voice and the vote" of the United States to oppose any financial assistance by each international financial institution, effectively eliminating assistance from the IMF and the World Bank entirely. Washington choked the Yugoslav Federal Government, while funding individual republics or political parties, for instance, in Croatia, the far right Hrvatska Demokratska Zajednica (HDZ). The 1991 Foreign Appro-

---

Michael Camdessus. Markovic asked the World Bank for 300 to 350 million dollars as a component of a billion dollar package designed to create a market economy system in Yugoslavia (*East European Markets* 20 October 1989). He said that Yugoslavia was in the process of paying the IMF 575 million dollars in 1989, but he added, "We're not going to receive a single dollar from them." He indicated that the IMF should lend more money to help promote his reform package (*East European Markets* 20 October 1989).

priations law demanded separate elections in each of the six republics, instead of countrywide elections and supported assistance to
"democratic parties and movements." In this sense, "democratic"
means anything that is not communist or socialist. However, Yugoslavian worker's self-management was a highly democratic system. Because of the empowerment of workers, this system would
be intolerable to the overseers of the U.S. economy in Washington
and New York. Section 599a of the 1991 Foreign Operations Appropriations Act stated, "Provided further, That this section shall
not apply to the assistance intended to support democratic parties and movements, emergency or humanitarian assistance, or the
furtherance of human rights" (Foreign Operations Appropriations
for 1991 P.L 101-513 1990). Additionally, the law, referred to as the
Nickles Amendment, barred Yugoslavia from raising money in the
international financial markets. Gow (1991, p. 306) writes that the
withdrawal of U.S. support was tacit approval for secession:

> The removal of support for Yugoslavia as a whole appeared to
> prepare the way for recognition of individual republics as in-
> dependent states, which was implicit in U.S. Secretary of State
> James Baker's announcement that future assistance would be on
> a case by case basis.

Croatian nationalists saw U.S. aid as support for their secession.
A senior Croat said, "We hope that soon the Americans will give
the democratic republics aid, then we will be getting *de facto* recognition" (Gow 1991, p. 306). The U.S. ostensibly changed its public
policy when it became increasingly clear that aid and recognition
were being associated. However, the Nickles Amendment remained
active policy. In addition to violating the U.N. Charter, the United
States, Germany (and other Western nations), and the secessionist
parties in Yugoslavia were violating the terms of the 1975 Helsinki
Accords, to which they were all signatories to, and which prohibited secession by force, the interference in the domestic affairs of
sovereign countries, and the inviolability of frontiers (Organization
for Security and Co-operation in Europe 2008).

Warren Zimmerman, U.S. Ambassador to Yugoslavia 1989-
1992, writes that Tudjman's party — the HDZ, whose leadership

were guests in the White House, reminded Serbs of the Croatian fascists from World War II that had tortured and killed hundreds of thousands of Serbs in concentration camps:

> There is a tragic subtext to the racist attitude toward Serbs that Tudjman tolerated within his party. During World War II Croatia was a Nazi puppet state under Hitler's control. . . . [T] he Croatian fascists of that period — the Ustaše — committed unspeakable atrocities against Serbs in Croatia and Bosnia. In this Yugoslav civil war, Serbs Croats, Muslims, Gypsies, and Jews were all victimized, but no group suffered more than the Serbs. By changing street names that had previously honored victims of fascism and reviving the traditional Croatian flag and coat of arms last used during the 1941–1945 Ustaše dictatorship, the Croatian government contributed to the resurrection of this grotesque period in the minds of the Serbs (Zimmerman 1996, p. 75).

Markovic lobbied to promote nationwide federal elections to reaffirm federal authority and increase stability but was opposed by republican nationalists holding power in several republics.[33] On June 25, 1991, Croatia and Slovenia unilaterally declared their independence from the Federal Republic of Yugoslavia. In Croatia, Serbs were the second largest ethnic community, numbering 581,663 (12.2%), according to the 1991 census (Klemencič 1996, p. 109). The Croatians held a referendum in which the Croatian majority voted to secede from Yugoslavia, but Croatia's Serbian minority, the "Krajina" Serbs, voted to remain with Yugoslavia (Hupchick 2004, p. 440). The Serbian opposition, in addition to other socioeconomic factors, inflamed ethnic rivalries and lead to violence. Johnson (2007, pp. 59-60) writes of accounts of murder, torture, and persecution of Serbs in Croatia:

---

33 Yugoslavia's first multiparty elections were scheduled for December 1990; however, they were to be held only on the republic level and not on the federal level. Since the 1974 constitution, each republic held a veto over federal policy. Slovenia vetoed any possible federal elections. At the start of 1990, a poll conducted by Delo found that 52 percent of Slovenes favored "a confederation association with Yugoslavia," 28 percent favored complete secession, and 8 percent liked the system as it had been (Bookman 1994, p. 176).

At the outset, there was the murder and mutilation of wounded and captured members of the JNA. Then we learned of executions of Serb villagers at Vukovar, Borovo, Naselje, Gospic, and elsewhere. It was the instruments of murder that shocked the most: hatchets, knives, strangulation devices, and tools to gouge out eyes and others to mutilate male genital organs. The ethnic cleansing began almost at once with expulsion orders with crisis committees amid threats and intimidation. By August 1992, Serbs had been evicted from some two hundred villages in western Slavonia alone, a process accompanied by looting and the destruction of property, as well as acts of violence against individuals.

The standard version put forth by the mainstream media in the West has always been that Serb atrocities from 1991-1995, during the Croatian and Bosnian Wars, were responsible for intervention by Western powers. In addition to ignoring mass atrocities committed against Serbs, mainstream accounts have all but ignored that fact that Western powers were deeply involved in the incitement of secession and civil war in Yugoslavia long before the wars in Croatia and Bosnia began. In 1991, Germany and Austria were the first and most ardent supporters of the break-up of Yugoslavia, and they successfully lobbied the European Community. The United States played a behind-the-scenes role early on. Slovenia's and Croatia's unilateral declarations of independence, in violation of the Helsinki Accords, and the taking up of arms against the federal government to defend those declarations, were contrary to accepted international norms. Nonetheless, those declarations would have amounted to two small conflicts and been resolved properly through peaceful negotiations had some Western governments not inflamed the situation.

Germany's Role

Christopher Bennett, a Slovenian, writes that for German Foreign Minister Hans Dietrich Genscher, "the issue [of Croatian and Slovenian independence] became a personal crusade" (Bennett 1995, p. 178). "Since Germany was unable to deploy troops for constitutional reasons, the most Genscher could offer Croatia was international recognition and this rapidly became the goal of German diplomacy" (Bennett 1995, pp. 178-179). Richard Holbrooke, U.S. Ambassador to Germany from 1993–1994, writes, "For months Germany had been pressing the E.C. [European Community] and the United States to recognize Croatia" (Holbrooke 1998, p. 31). Cyrus Vance, former U.S. Secretary of State under President Jimmy Carter, was appointed chief U.N. mediator for Yugoslavia and the E.C. asked former British Foreign Secretary Lord Carrington to lead a mediation effort for settlement to the Balkan crisis. For Vance and Carrington, mediation proved difficult as external forces were sabotaging any efforts at a peaceful solution. According to Holbrooke (1998, p.31), "Vance and Carrington opposed the German position vigorously. They both told me later that they had warned their old friend and colleague German Foreign Minister Hans Dietrich Genscher, in the strongest possible terms, that recognizing Croatia would trigger a chain reaction culminating in a war in Bosnia." Vance and Carrington foretold that if Croatia declared independence, Bosnia would follow, the considerable Serb minority in Bosnia would reject living in a state ruled by the Muslims, and that would trigger a rebellion by that Serb minority. One Yugoslavian said that, during the breakdown of the federal system, each ethnic group would pose the question: "Why should I be a minority in your state, when you can be a minority in mine?" (Holbrooke 1998, p. 31). The dream of the seven decades of multiethnic Yugoslavia was coming to an end as Germany and Austria led the charge for homogenous ethnic states in the Balkans.

The German government appeared to be uninterested in negotiations and on a mission to recognize Slovenia and Croatia no matter the cost, whether it meant bloodshed and suffering for the people of Yugoslavia or destroying the new European "unity" following the recently signed Maastricht Treaty. Holbrooke (1999, p. 31) writes, "Genscher, the senior Foreign Minister in Europe, ignored the warning of his old friends. Uncharacteristically flexing Germany's muscles during a critical foreign ministers meeting in Brussels in mid-December 1991, he told his colleagues that if they did not support him, Germany would simply recognize Croatia unilaterally."

Genscher's hard-line position persuaded his European colleagues that European unity was more desirable than opposing Genscher's position. Holbrook (1998, p. 31) continues, "Faced with a threat of a public break in European 'unity' just when the historic Maastricht Treaty was proclaiming the dawn of a new, unified Europe — a treaty whose prime mover had been German Chancellor Helmut Kohl — the other European countries yielded to Genscher." Genscher's colleagues requested Germany to wait to recognize Slovenia and Croatia, but Germany went ahead and granted recognition in December 1991.

While Germany aided Slovenian and Croatian nationalists, it was experiencing extreme levels of xenophobia and racism at home. The German government was explicitly tolerating and encouraging xenophobic and racist attacks in Germany. In 1995, Human Rights Watch Helsinki published a 55 page report titled, "'Germany for Germans' Xenophobia and racist Violence in Germany." The report lambasted the German Authorities' response to the 800 percent increase in attacks on foreigners after unification from 1990-1992. The report stated, "Human Rights Watch/Helsinki (HRW) found at the time that the German State's response to the violence had significantly contributed to an environment in which anti-foreigner sentiments flourished and appeared to be tolerated by the state" (Human Rights Watch 1995). In October 1992, HRW/Helsinki, then Helsinki Watch, had published a similar report "on xenophobia and racist violence in Germany" that "identified serious problems in a number of areas: the police response to violence against foreigners; the prosecutors' response to xenophobic crime; the judiciary's response to trials of skinheads and others who attack foreigners; and the federal government's response to the rise in violence aimed at foreigners" (Helsinki Watch 1992, p. 1). It concluded that Germany was confronted with a crisis of intolerance at all levels within its own borders:

> Germany is currently confronted with a political and social crisis that has profound consequences for German citizens, as well as for the foreigners who seek refuge within its borders. . . . Rioting skinheads throwing Molotov cocktails at refugee shelters,

onlookers applauding and cheering, slogans such as "foreigners out" and "Germany for Germans," inevitably recall images of Nazi terror during the Third Reich. Physical injury, fear and humiliation have become a daily experience for foreigners in unified Germany (Helsinki Watch 1992, p. 1).

It seems logical that a government so rife with problems of ethnic intolerance should not have been leading the agenda to create a peaceful solution to conflict in a multiethnic country in danger of fracturing along ethnic fault lines. Germany became the banner holder for nationalists seeking mono-ethnic independent states. Utkin (1999, p. 10) writes that Genscher disguised the principle of ethnic self-determination among humanitarian rhetoric:

> Genscher hid the principle of self-determination among humanitarian principles, but it was clear to Europe and the world who was the most stalwart pillar of national self-determination in its "pure" form. These countries thereby repudiated the experience of the multiethnic United States, France, England, and others in favor of the principle of Germanic ethnocentrism. Germany's ethnocentric policy became the banner of Germany's ethnically self-affirming European partners. The newly independent countries were incapable even of considering the official bilingualism practiced by Belgium, Finland, and Canada and other tokens of respect for minorities.

Germany viewed Yugoslavia as part of *Mitteleuropa* — their natural sphere of influence. The *Bundesnachrichtendienst* (BND), the German intelligence agency, had been operating in the Balkans for decades and encouraging ideas of secession to grow in Yugoslavia, and they played a significant role in instigating the wars of secession in Yugoslavia.

In late September 1991, the U.N. Security Council imposed an arms embargo on all of Yugoslavia, which included the secessionist republics.[34] In February 1993, Germany called for the Bosnian Muslims to be armed, which vexed Paris and London (Doughty

---

34 UNSC resolution 713 states: *Decides*, under Chapter VII of the Charter of the United Nations, that all States shall, for the purposes of establishing peace and stability in Yugoslavia, immediately implement a general and complete embargo on all deliveries of weapons and military equipment to Yugoslavia until the Council decides otherwise follow-

1993, p. 10). The Clinton Administration and high ranking members of Congress, in both parties, were raising the issue of lifting the embargo to create more military balance between the Serbs and the Bosnian Muslims.[35] Mediator Lord Owen said that arming the Bosnian Muslims would be akin to "pouring oil on the flames" (Doughty 1993, p. 10). Britain and France were concerned for their peacekeeping forces acting under U.N. authorization in Bosnia and maintained that lifting the embargo would result in a substantial escalation in the fighting. They also indicated that the Muslims and Croats were responsible for the recent outbreaks in fighting, and not the Serbs (Doughty 1993, p. 10). French Foreign Minister Alain Juppé said that lifting the embargo to arm the Bosnian Muslims would "mean the internationalization of the conflict and a general conflagration in the Balkans" (Cohen 1993, p. A15). He warned that if that took place, France would withdraw all four thousand of its

---

ing consultation between the Secretary-General and the Government of Yugoslavia (United Nations 1991b).

35 The attempt to use Article 51 as a self-defense justification came from Republicans and Democrats alike. Bob Dole, U.S. Senate Minority Leader said, "Extending the arms embargo to Bosnia violates Bosnia's fundamental right to self-defense — a right that is incorporated in Article 51 of the U.N. Charter. . . ." (Dole 1994). Democratic Senator Joseph Biden of Delaware issued a press release that said, "As every student of international law and of the United Nations knows, Article 51 of the U.N. Charter grants every member state the right of self-defense" (Biden 1995). Democratic Senator Daniel Patrick Moynihan of New York tried to make his case that the UN Charter allowed for countries to violate unilaterally a UN embargo out of self-defense. He said that this type of situation "was specifically contemplated as a problem when the [U.N.] Charter was drafted . . . and that is why Article 51 says 'nothing in this Charter shall interfere with the inherent right of individual or collective self-defense'" (Sawyer 1994, p. A7). Moynihan's argument for Bosnian self-defense misses the basic observation that the Bosnian war a civil war, not an attack on the Bosnians from a foreign country. The Charter prohibits the interference in the internal affairs of state. If the Security Council deems a situation within a country to be a threat to international peace and security or if there is an internal situation in which the Council can be of assistance, within the spirit of the Charter, then action may be taken, but it must be authorized by the Council.

---

peacekeepers.[36]Unlike France, Germany did not have peacekeepers in Yugoslavia. It had been playing another role since fighting began: covertly shipping weapons to Croatia. Illegal weapons were shipped from a variety of countries, but the most notable were Germany and Iran. Numerous reports had surfaced of Croatian soldiers or militias wearing German helmets from the former GDR and carrying German weapons. The publication *Defense and Foreign Affairs Strategic Policy*, the official journal of the International Strategic Studies Association, claimed in an October 1992 report, that it "uncovered a widespread pattern of arms shipments which have been allowed to cross into Croatia and Bosnia with the tacit approval (and sometimes, apparently, direct support) of the governments of Germany and Austria, and possibly other states" (*Defense and Foreign Affairs Strategic Policy* Oct. 1992). The report stated, "War in the former Yugoslav republics is being fueled by a massive and complex pattern of shipments to Croatia and Bosnia-Herzegovina, funded and organized by Germany" (*Defense and Foreign Affairs Strategic Policy* Oct. 1992). While Germany refused to supply troops to UNPROFOR peacekeeping mission, stating such an action violated its constitution, the Germans provided intelligence, sensitive equipment, and arms to the Croatian forces. In 1994, *Jane's Intelligence Review* documented illegal German covert activity fueling the war in Yugoslavia:

> Germany had reportedly supplied some restricted U.S. items of airborne reconnaissance and other sensitive equipment to the SIS. As regards SIS in Germany, the BfV [Federal Office for the Protection of the Constitution] and other German intelligence services have long turned a blind eye to them, particularly as regards the illegal Croatian procurement of armaments locally, including surplus military equipment from the old East German

---

36 France and Germany had sharp divisions on European policy, and adding to this tension, their differing perspectives on the arms embargo were brought to the foreground in late June in Copenhagen at the European Community's meeting, where German Chancellor Helmut Kohl expressed his support for lifting the embargo to allow weapon shipments to the Bosnian Muslims; and after the meeting, Juppe responded by declaring, "It is easy for countries that do not actually have troops on the ground to give such advice" (Cohen 1993, p. D2).

Army in violation of the present U.N. arms embargo against the former Yugoslavia. As for other major Western intelligence services, none has gone so far as Germany in Croatia (Milivojevic 1994, p. 408).

The Belgrade daily *Borba* reported in November 1993 that Croatia had recently bought a number of MiG-21 and MiG-29 aircraft from the former East German Army *(Yugoslav Telegraph Service* 1993, EE/1849/C). The Belgrade daily also reported that, according to British sources, Croatia had bought 35 such aircraft and, according to American sources, the figure was nine. The report stated that the Croatians were buying tanks from Germany, "which wants to rid itself of the former East Germany arsenal and switch to the standard Western technology" *(Yugoslav Telegraph Service* 1993, EE/1849/C).

Supporting nationalist movements and recognizing the unilateral declarations of independence in Slovenia, Croatia, and then Bosnia, the West, led by Germany, disregarded the aspirations of Yugoslavians, across ethnic lines, wanting to live in a pluralistic society. This is especially true for Croatia and Bosnia. Barratt-Brown (2005, p. 143) argues that the recognition of the declarations of independence ignored those yearning for a pluralistic society. He writes, "It thus neglected the interests of those who as Serbs wished to continue to live in Yugoslavia, and had expressed this wish in referenda. It also negated the wishes of those from all communities who wished to live in a pluralistic society." In July 1991, 50,000 people in Sarajevo marched to voice their support for a unified Yugoslavia.

> I heard of this [the march] through our friend Nada Kraigher's granddaughter Nina, who had been active in organizing the march, herself a Slovene married to a Bosnian Muslim. The most harrowing story of such cross-communal relations in Sarajevo was that of the young lovers from different communities who were caught in the cross-fire while wading one night through Miljacka and were found [the] next day dead in each other's arms under the shallow running waters of the river (Barratt-Brown 2005, p. 143).

Mikloj-Nikola Simijanovic, an artist from Vukovar, Croatia, said that he loved his life in his hometown until 1990. He recalled Vukovar as being one of the most affluent cities in Yugoslavia with a vibrant cultural life. However, he said that life changed in 1990 when Zagreb tried to fix the local elections in favor of only Croatians. The problem became much worse when local Croatian extremists obtained weapons, and "Non-Croats were intimidated and fired from jobs" (Johnson 2007, p.39). The multi-ethnic and decentralized socialist country was on the brink of destruction as Washington and its NATO allies prepared to accelerate its policy of destruction.

Oil on Fire

In the early stages of the conflict, the United States took a more duplicitous position, supporting Yugoslav unity in rhetoric while working to disintegrate the country through a policy of economic shock therapy and support for extremist secessionist elements within the individual nations. In its usual anti-communist position and with a lack of understanding of the Yugoslav reality, the U.S. Congress and key government officials supported the "democratic opposition," even though that group was comprised of right-wing nationalists bent on shattering the country. The United States quietly opposed the recognition of Slovenia and Croatia by the European Community (EC). Zimmerman (1996, p. 177) described the instructions on recognition from Washington as "perfunctory . . . enough to show we had done something, but not enough to produce results . . . weak and nuanced, [designed] mainly to avoid ruffling the Croatian Community in the United States"

In early 1994, Croatian nationalist leader Franco Tudjman asked the United States government if arms could be shipped through Croatia to the Bosnian government (Bonner & Weiner 1996, p. A1). These weapons included significant armaments from Iran, which sought to arm the Bosnian Muslims. Bosnia is a land-locked territory and any ground shipments would have to traverse Croatia. The American Ambassador to Croatia, Peter W. Galbraith, relayed the message to Tudjman, with President Clinton's approval, that there were "no instructions" (Bonner & Weiner 1996, p. A1). The phrase *no instructions* is diplomatic talk signaling that a government will stand aside, and it is acceptable to proceed with a plan of action. Tudjman did not understand the meaning of the message, so he asked Charles Redman, U.S. special envoy in the Balkans, who informed him that the United States had no objections to the weapon shipments (Bonner & Weiner 1996, p. A1). The arms flowed in and the Croatian government seized half of the weapons bound for Bosnia.

In November 1994, the Clinton Administration, much to the surprise of its European allies, announced that the United States would no longer enforce the U.N. arms embargo. This was known as the "green light policy." European countries, with significant peacekeeping forces in Bosnia — notably France and Britain, immediately criticized the announcement.[37] The United States Navy no longer interfered with ships carrying arms, and ceased intelligence sharing with its European partners on weapon shipments to Croatia and Bosnia. Bosnia had been receiving covert weapons shipments, largely via air drops; however, the "green light policy" signaled to Islamic countries, intent on further arming the Bosnian Muslims, weapons could be shipped with the assent of the United States. The U.S. did not attempt to quell the violence in Bosnia or act as a neutral mediator or peace enforcer, but rather, it endeavored to arm the Bosnian government, so it could acquire territory held by the Serbs. A ranking NATO officer told the *New York Times*, "The United States has just taken sides" (Whitney, 1994, p. 1.1).[38]

The U.S. not only allowed the flow of weapons into the Balkans, it sent arms directly to Bosnia itself in January 1995, employing covert air drops. Those at Tuzla, in northern Bosnia, observed by members of the nearby stationed U.N. Nordic Battalion, were

---

37 According to the *New York Times*, British Foreign Secretary Douglas Hurd said, "It is a worry because this is a mandatory resolution of the Security Council and an agreed policy of the alliance" (Whitney 1994, p. 1.1). The French Foreign Ministry stated that its Foreign Minister, Alain Juppe, called his American counterpart, U.S. Secretary of State Warren Christopher, and that Juppé "conveyed the French Government's deep worries about this unilateral decision, which we [France] can only regret" (Whitney, 1994, p. 1.1).

38 From the start of the conflict, the United States and its European allies had taken sides by opposing the Serbs; however, the "green light policy" was explicit.

the "most well documented" (McDonald 2001). The illegal drops included stinger surface-to-air missiles, anti-tank guided weapons, night vision goggles, and Motorola radio sets "for large scale offensive operations" (McDonald 2001). Senior U.N. peacekeeping commanders in Bosnia clashed with NATO over air drops to the Bosnian Army. In February, about 20 U.N. observers witnessed the clandestine drops on four occasions: February 10, 12, 17, and 23. The British head of G2, the UNPROFOR intelligence unit, also witnessed the drops. The U.N. observers said that they heard "transport type aircraft of C-130 or like size" near the West Tuzla airbase between 6 p.m. and 9 p.m. The observers said the aircraft, escorted by fighter jets, "appeared to be making a lower level parachute drop, a maneuver performed only by U.S., British or French air forces," *the Independent* of London reported (Dowden 1995, p. 10). Lieutenant General Bertrand de Lapresle, the U.N. commander in the former Yugoslavia, said that the February 10 and 12 air drops were evaluated to have been "two clandestine re-supplies" of "high-value/high technology guided missiles or perhaps surface to air missiles" (Dowden 1995).

NATO denied the U.N. observer's and ground commander's reports of clandestine air drops near Tuzla, and these denials "infuriated" U.N. commanders. NATO had universally accepted all U.N. reports in Bosnia as accurate, yet it made an extra effort to discredit the reports on covert weapons shipments, documented by U.N. staff and commanders.[39] American officials did acknowledge, however, that it was against U.S. interests to keep the embargo in place (Dowden 1995, p. 10). In addition to arming Croatia, the U.S. provided enormous amounts of intelligence: aerial reconnaissance, electronic intelligence, signal intelligence, and agents deployed in NGOs, U.N. agencies, and military agencies. The intelligence was not supplied to NATO or the U.N. but only to Croatia (McDonald 2001).

---

39 Senior U.S. officials rejected that U.S. aircraft were involved, and said that if these air drops had indeed occurred, perhaps they were from an Islamic country such as Iran. One official rejected the suggestion that Turkey, a NATO member, was involved saying that idea was "dubious."

In 1991, the Croatian forces were weak — sometimes described as a "tin pot army"; but by 1995, they had arguably the strongest army in the region. This transformation occurred while under an international arms embargo. In 1995, Croatian forces drove the Serbian minority from what they claimed to be Croatia, the territory designated to them in 1941, under the protection of Hitler and Mussolini. The Croats captured western Slavonia and the Krajina region from the Serbs, driving 200,000 Croatian Serbs from their homes, in what Croatia dubbed "Operation Storm." The BBC reported that "a team of retired U.S. Officers planned the bloody 'liberation' of the Krajina and the subsequent invasion of western Bosnia by the Croatian Army in the summer of 1995" (McDonald 2001). The Croatian military contracted Military Professional Resources Inc. (MPRI), a private contractor comprised of ex-Pentagon and U.S. military officials, to train the Croatian Army. The objective of "Operation Storm" was to "ethnically cleanse" Serbs from the Krajina region.

In 2002, retired U.S. Air Force colonel George Jatras wrote a letter to the *Washington Times* in which he said, "without U.S. military aid and technology, 'Operation Storm' may have not been successful" (Jatras 2002, p. B02). U.S. air strikes on August 4, 1995, against Serb missile sites, as reported by the *NAVY Times*, showed that they were in the same area where the Croatians were attacking as they began "Operation Storm." The air strikes were said to have been initiated because of a request by Pakistani U.N. peacekeepers who reported Croatian artillery rounds hitting close to their post. Despite that, U.S. aircraft targeted and hit Serb positions instead of Croatian targets (*Navy Times* 25 August 1995, p. 2). Col. Jatras writes that he called the office of Sen. John W. Warner, a Virginia Republican, and asked him, "Why, when we claimed to be neutral, U.S. aircraft had put in an air strike against Serb facilities in support of the Croatian offensive in Krajina?" (Jatras 2002, p. B02).

In 2005, ten years after "Operation Storm," Amnesty International (AI) issued a public statement entitled "Croatia: 'Operation Storm' — still no justice ten years later on." The human rights organization decried the lack of justice and accountability for the crimes committed against the Serbs of Croatia. Amnesty stated, "Impunity must end for crimes committed during Operations 'Flash' and 'Storm' as well as for killings, 'disappearances,' and torture committed against Croatian Serbs in the first phase of the conflict" (Amnesty International 2005). The AI statement summarized "Operation Storm":

> During and after these military offenses, some 200, 000 Croatian Serbs, including the entire Serb army, fled to the neighboring Federal Republic of Yugoslavia and areas of Bosnia and Herzegovina under Bosnian Serb control. In the aftermath of the operations members of the Croatian Army and police murdered, tortured, and forcibly expelled Croatian Serb civilians who had remained in the area as well as members of the withdrawing Croatian Serb armed forces (Amnesty International 2005).

U.N. Secretary General Boutros Boutros-Ghali made it clear in his May 30, 1995 report to the Security Council, what had become obvious, that the U.S. backed Bosnian Army was organizing and launching attacks from in and around U.N. "safe areas:"

> In recent months [Bosnian] government forces have considerably increased their military activity in and around most safe areas, and many of them, including Sarajevo, Tuzla, and Bihac, have been incorporated into the broader military campaign of the [Bosnian] government's side (United Nations 1995).

> The headquarters and the logistics installations of the Fifth Corps of the [Bosnian] government army are located in the town of Bihac and those of the Second Corps in the town of Tuzla (United Nations 1995).

> The government also maintains a substantial number of troops in Srebrenica (in this case a violation of a demilitarization agreement), Gorazde and Zepa, while Sarajevo is the location of the General Command of the government army and other military installations. There is also an ammunition factory in Gorazde (United Nations 1995).

> The Bosnian Serb forces' reaction to offensives launched by the [Bosnian] government army from safe areas have generally been to respond against military targets within those areas (United Nations 1995).

On August 28, 1995, a blast in a Sarajevo marketplace killed 37 people, and NATO blamed the Serbs (NATO 2002). The perpetrator of the blast remained disputed by some experts, who said that it was impossible for Serb artillery to have conducted the act of terrorism. In addition to the marketplace bombing, the Bosnian Serbs were accused of shelling U.N. safe areas. For three weeks, from August 30 to September 20, 1995, NATO launched air strikes against the Bosnian Serbs under "Operation Deliberate Force. According to NATO, they flew 3515 sorties and dropped 1026 bombs, attacking Bosnian Serb positions.

By illegally arming the Bosnian government, the U.S. and other states had made the "safe areas" much more dangerous, especially since they were not only places for civilians to avoid harm but for the Bosnian government to organize and launch attacks. Safe areas were used, at the expense of civilians, for one side to gain a strategic advantage and a public relations victory. The U.S. and NATO manipulated the Bosnian government army's positioning in and near safe areas to demonize one side to the conflict — the Bosnian Serbs; this strategy was employed to create a perception of legitimacy for the air bombardment against almost exclusively Bosnian Serb targets. On the ground atrocities against civilians were conducted by all sides: the Croatians, the Bosnian Serbs, and the Bosnian government. Yet, U.S. and NATO forces targeted only one side: the Bosnian Serbs.

Retired U.S. General Charles G. Boyd USAF, Deputy Commander in Chief of U.S. European Command from 1992 to July 1995, writes in *Foreign Affairs* that what the Western media calls Serbian aggression is merely an effort to hang on to land it has occupied for more than three centuries:

> Much of what Zagreb calls the occupied territories is in fact land held by Serbs for more than three centuries. . . . [T]he same is true of most of Serb land in Bosnia, what the Western media frequently refers to as the 70 percent of Bosnia seized by rebel Serbs. There were only 500,000 fewer Serbs than Muslims in Bosnia at independence, with more rural Serbs tending towards larger landholdings. In short, the Serbs are not trying to conquer

new territory, but merely to hold on to what was already theirs (Boyd 1995, p. 22).

An urgent need for neutral mediation and peacekeeping existed in Croatia and Bosnia, to bring an end to the violence and to prevent a further escalation of the fighting. However, nothing in the U.N. Charter supports arming one side of a civil conflict so that party can further its strategic goals over its adversaries. U.S. Air Force General (Retired) Charles Boyd (1995, p. 22) writes that the Bosnian Serbs were trying to achieve the same general goal as the Croats and Muslims, but their legitimate aspirations were opposed at every turn by the U.S. and NATO:

> In this atmosphere of fear, uncertainty, and resurgent nationalism, first the Croatians [with Western support] and then the Bosnian Serbs — with Serbian support took up arms to do what international recognition [and taking up arms] had done for the Croats of Croatia and the Muslims of Bosnia: ensure that they would not be a minority in a state perceived to be hostile. What is frequently referred to as rampant Serb nationalism and the creation of greater Serbia has often been the same volatile mixture of fear, opportunism, and historied myopia that seems to motivate patriots everywhere in the Balkans.

While at Dayton, Serbian President Slobodan Milosevic turned to General Wesley Clark during lunch and said, "Well, General Clark, you must be pleased that NATO won this war [last round of fighting in Bosnia]." General Clark replied, "Mr. President, NATO didn't even fight this war. You lost it to the Croats and Muslims." Milosevic looked at Clark and responded, "No. It was your NATO, your bombs and missiles, your high technology that defeated us. We Serbs never had a chance against you" (Clark 2001, pp. 67-68).

In November 1995, at the Wright-Patterson Air Force Base, near Dayton, Ohio, the U.S. hosted peace talks, which lasted twenty days. Richard Holbrooke was the principal negotiator. According to Holbrooke's own book he tried to cheat Milosevic at Dayton and renege on an already decided-upon land agreement. Holbrooke and his team had asked John Menzies, who would become U.S. Ambassador to Bosnia-Herzegovina in 1996, to come up with the figures of the gains the Bosnians had made during the negotiations.[40] When Holbrooke saw the charts, it was clear that the figures on the charts exceeded by four percent the formally agreed upon percentage ratio of 51–49 in favor of the Bosnian Federation:

> The posters contained one particularly sensitive item. Measuring the territorial concessions that Milosevic had already made, the Defense Mapping Agency team had determined that 55 percent of Bosnia was now conceded to the Federation.... [U]nder the 1994 Contact Group Plan, all five Contact Group Foreign Ministers and the leaders of all three countries had formally agreed to a 51–49 split of Bosnian territory between the Federation and the Bosnian Serbs.... [W]e decided to see if we could retain this higher percentage.... [W]e knew that if Milosevic objected, we would have little choice to fall back to the 51–49 formula, given the prior commitments of the United States and the four other nations of the Contact Group. Tony Lake had reaffirmed this as a core American position during his August trip to the European capitals before the start of our shuttle, and it has been included in the September 9 Geneva agreement (Holbrooke 1998, pp. 294-295).

Despite knowing that he was breaking a formal agreement, Holbrooke and his team decided to attempt to deceive Milosevic to turn 51–49 into 55–45. Holbrooke hoped the Bosnians would be so happy with the "dramatic percentage figures" that they would quickly agree to the remaining items left to negotiate before Milosevic realized he had been cheated. "While the Bosnians were fascinated with our charts," Holbrooke writes, "they continued to argue over minor issues." At Milosevic's request, he met with Alija Izetbegovic, the Bosnian leader, to discuss Sarajevo and to find a solution to come to an agreement, but Milosevic saw the charts "peeking out from behind the couch" with big letters reading, "FEDERATION TERRITORY INCREASED FROM 50% to 55% DURING DAYTON TALKS" (Holbrooke 1998, p. 295). He immediately went to Holbrooke, who was in his room, and said, "You tricked me. You didn't tell me that the percentage was no longer 51–49. I asked you,

---

40 Menzies collaborated with the graphics division at Wright-Patterson to produce charts detailing those figures.

but you didn't reply. I saw your charts. How can I trust you?" (Holbrooke 1998, p. 295).

Holbrooke's accounts of Dayton showed Milosevic as being the peacemaker and indicated the frustration of the mediators with the Washington-backed Bosnians unwillingness to seek peace:

> Do you think Izetbegovic even wants a deal? Carl asked. It was a question that Warren Christopher had also been asking. "I'm never quite sure," I replied, "Sometimes he seems to want revenge more than peace — but he can't have both." Chris Hill, normally highly supportive of the Bosnians, exploded in momentary anger and frustration. "These people are impossible to help," he said. It was a telling statement from a man who had devoted years of his life to the search for ways to help create a Bosnian state (Holbrooke 1998, p. 302).

Carl Bildt crossed paths with Milosevic between the buildings and Milosevic was "desperate." "Give me anything, rocks, swamps, hills — anything, as long as it gets us to 49–51," Milosevic said, according to Holbrooke (1998, p. 302). When the agreement was finalized, Milosevic had tears in his eyes. After the Dayton Accords were signed, Chicago-based Amoco (American Oil Company) and other Western firms started initial exploration for oil in Bosnia (Chossudovsky 1997, p. 258). In 2008, Western multinationals confirmed the presence of large quantities of oil and began intense exploration near Tuzla, where U.S. army bases are now situated.

CHAPTER SEVEN: KOSOVO

The 1974 Yugoslavian Constitution accorded Kosovo virtual equality with the other republics. Kosovo Albanians acquired nearly universal control over provincial and local administration, which resulted in widespread discrimination against Kosovo's Serbian population. Jatras (2000, p. 22) writes that perhaps hundreds of thousands of Serbs were driven from Kosovo in the 1970s and 1980s:

> Tens, perhaps hundreds of thousands of Serbs left during the 1970s and 1980s in the face of pervasive discrimination and the refusal of authorities to protect them from ethnic violence. The resulting shift in the ethnic balance that accelerated during this period is the main claim ethnic Albanians now make to exclusive ownership of Kosovo.[41]

The rise of Slobodan Milosevic to power can be partially credited to his rhetoric in defense of Kosovo's Serb minority. In 1989, he downgraded Kosovo's autonomy to its pre-1974 constitution level but did not revoke it. From 1989 until violence erupted in Kosovo, eight years elapsed, but at no point was there a Serbian plot to carry out ethnic cleansing in Kosovo. In 1997, the Kosovo Liberation

---

[41] Jatras (2000, p. 23) refers to Serbian life in Kosovo before 1989 as "the oppressive character of pre-1989 ethnic Albanian rule in Kosovo."

Army (KLA) decided to take the issue of autonomy and turn it into a violent campaign against the state.

"Dubious sources, including drug money" bankrolled the KLA. In 1999, an investigation by *The Times* of London reported "police forces in three Western European countries and Europol, the European police authority, are separately investigating growing evidence that drug money is funding the KLA's leap from obscurity to power" (Boyes & Wright 1999). The *Washington Times* reported that the KLA bought "sophisticated weapons with cash from an "independent tax" levied against expatriates and from profits of illicit drugs and prostitution" (Seper 1999, p, A1). The publication also referred to information obtained in intelligence documents that "described the KLA as a terrorist organization that has financed much of its war effort with money sent to rebels by ethnic Albanians throughout Western Europe and the United States, and through profits from the sale of drugs, mainly heroin" (Seper 1999, p. A1). In addition, the KLA reportedly received arms shipments from both the United States and Islamic fundamentalists, sometimes via Bosnia. Journalist and author John Pilger (2007, p. 278) writes that the KLA was "funded and armed by the United States — and al-Qaeda. Weapons received by the Bosnians to fight the Serbs were shipped from Bosnia by the Stranka Demokratske Akcije (SDA) to the KLA." U.S. Congressman Trent Franks (U.S. House of Representatives 2005, sect. 42) of Arizona, a Republican, describes the SDA as "the radical Islamist Muslim SDA Party in Bosnia, a party that has had, since its foundation [1990], strong links with al-Qaeda, [and] numerous other terrorist organizations..." According to Schindler (2007, p. 267), a professor at the U.S. Naval War College, SDA support for the KLA was "underreported" but a story that was "well known to experts." Schindler writes, "NATO peacekeepers in Bosnia uncovered more than one cache of weapons bound for Kosovo; no less, Western troops serving in Kosovo after the NATO intervention found weapons and munitions bearing clear Bosnian Muslim markings. This was another story it was in neither NATO's nor Western media's interest to over-publicize" (2007, p. 267).

The KLA carried out attacks for more than a year before the Yugoslav police and paramilitary units responded with a "concerted" effort (Parenti 2000, p, 102). In early 1998, the attacks increased. From January through March 1998 the KLA intensified its attacks on Serbian targets in Kosovo: carrying out a program of assassinations against Serbian officials; bombarding police; and employing terrorism against government buildings, sites, and Serbian civilians (Layne 2000, p. 13). According to former CIA official Wes Johnson, Yugoslav sources indicated that almost a thousand KLA actions took place in the first half of 1998:

> ...from January to July, 887 actions took place during which forty-four policemen and sixty-six civilians died. Some ninety-six policemen and thirty-eight civilians were seriously wounded. And, 171 civilians had been kidnapped — 125 Serbs and Montenegrins, thirty-seven Albanians, six Roma, one Yugoslav Muslim, and one each from Bulgaria and Macedonia. Of these, fifteen were killed, seven escaped, thirty-two were released, and 118 remain missing (Johnson 2007, p. 398).

In summer 1998, Serbian forces were drawn into the countryside seeking to thwart the KLA's terrorist activities. According to Kosovo Albanian sources, about two thousand lives were lost on both sides, while Yugoslavian sources numbered the deaths at eight hundred. The KLA sought to enkindle a harsh response to turn the Kosovar population completely against the FRY, thus gaining their support. Their other goal was to incite international opinion against the FRY and to draw Western powers into the conflict.

Yugoslav authorities recorded thousands of attacks against citizens and FRY authorities, including the police, state officials, and soldiers. The FRY records show 152 citizens killed in the first ten months of 1998: 68 Albanians, 37 Serbs and Montenegrins, 3 Gypsies and 42 people with unidentified identity: "The murders were committed in cruel ruthless ways, often in front of peasants, in order to scare the population and in order to make them participate in the terrorist actions" (Laughland 2007, p.20). The KLA used egregious tactics to provoke Belgrade. In 2005, the International Criminal Tribunal for the former Yugoslavia (ICTY) indicted Ramush Haradinaj, Prime Minister of Kosovo in 1998, and his deputy, Idriz

Balaj. The indictment contained allegations of torture and extreme brutality committed in 1998. One such incident was the August 1998 torture and killing of a pro-Yugoslav Albanian:

> While detained, Sali Berisha's nose was cut off, in the presence of Idriz Balaj and two other KLA soldiers. Idriz Balaj cut each of the three men on their necks, arms and thighs, rubbed salt into the cuts of and sewed them up with a needle. Idriz Balaj then wrapped Zenun Gashi, Misin Berisha, and Sali Berisha in barbed wire and used an implement to drive the barbs of the wire into their flesh. Idriz Balaj also stabbed Zenun Gashi in the eye. The three men were then tied behind Idriz Balaj's vehicle and dragged away in the direction of Lake Radonjic/Radoniq. They have not been seen alive since this day and are presumed to have been killed (*ICTY Prosecutor v. Ramush Haradinaj, Idriz Balaj, Lahi Brahimaj*, indictment, 4 March, 2005 cited in Laughland 2007, p.21).

At the September 23 Security Council meeting, Mr. Lavrov of the Russian Federation said, "In violation of Security Council resolution 1160 (1998), material and financial support from abroad continues to be provided to Kosovo extremists, first and foremost from the territory of Albania, which is seriously destabilizing the situation and provoking tensions in Kosovo" (United Nations 1998b, p. 2). Lavrov said the draft resolution, Resolution 1999, "explicitly reaffirms the sovereignty and territorial integrity of the Federal Republic of Yugoslavia." He pointed out that the resolution "insists" that the Kosovo Albanian leadership condemn terrorism and use only peaceful means, that the resolution "condemns the continuing promotion from abroad of terrorist activities in Kosovo" (United Nations 1998b, p. 3). A declassified CIA document, dated September 29, 1998, and labeled "Top Secret" — obtained under the Freedom of Information Act — describes the KLA as the aggressive party and the Yugoslav army as responding defensively:

> UCK [KLA] command structure is intact, waiting for the VJ [Yugoslav Army] to withdraw and bent on attacking supply lines. . . . [T]here are 5–8 thousand UCK fighters in the hills. UCK morale remains strong, some supplies still getting through, but they remain short of ammo. There is evidence that the UCK is reinfiltrating some areas they lost earlier and this reinfiltra-

tion continues. . . . At this time, there is no indication the VJ plans anything beyond sweep operations where the UCK rears up. The VJ leadership probably hopes by sealing the borders the UCK will wither. UCK's challenge is to improve militarily, which they're addressing via reorganization, strengthening command structure, and getting better arms. Mr. Wilson was told to expect sporadic, low level guerilla attacks by the UCK, especially if the VJ pulls back off the major roads, but no major fighting. ['slowdown with winter weather'] [Name deleted] ended the brief by predicting that if the UCK successfully resupplies itself by next spring, combat between the Serbs and the Kosovo rebels will reconvene at this time (Central Intelligence Agency 2005).

In 1998 and in the first three months of 1999, the German Foreign Ministry informed the German Courts that they should reject applications of Kosovo asylum seekers because of a lack of persecution against ethnic Albanians. Numerous asylum seekers were denied from January to March 1999. A January court observation read, "An explicit political persecution of the Albanian population cannot be established, even in Kosovo. . . .The actions of the security forces are not directed to Kosovo Albanians as an ethically defined group but instead against military opponents and their real or supposed supporters" (Administrative Court, Trier, 12 January 1999, cited in Laughland 2007, p.23). Another observation from a German court on October 29, 1998 sheds similar light on the situation before the U.S.–NATO bombing began:

> The entire action of the Yugoslav military and police since February 1998 was directed against separatist activities and does not indicate the persecution of the whole group of Albanians, whether in Kosovo as a whole or in parts of the province...A state program of persecution directed against the whole ethnic group of Albanians has not existed and does not exist (Urteil des Bayerischen Verwaltungsgerichtshofs vom: 29, Oktober 1998, Az: 22 BA 94.34252 cited in Laughland 2007, p. 23).[42]

---

42 Similar observations were given by German courts on February 24 and March 11, 1999 (Urteil des Observerwaltungsgerichts Munster vom 24. February 1999, Az: 14 A 3840/94.A cited in Laughland 2007, p.23; Urteil des Observerwaltungsgerichts Munster vom 11. Marz 1999, Az: 13A 3894/94.A cited in Laughland 2007, p.23).

The United States publicly opposed independence for Kosovo while simultaneously opposing Belgrade's right to counter an armed guerilla force operating and carrying out terrorist attacks within the territory of the FRY, this despite the United States putting down its own domestic insurrections with unmerciful force. In 1993, the relatively minor insurrection of the Branch Davidians, who barricaded themselves in the Waco compound in Texas, paled in comparison to the widespread terrorism and atrocities of the KLA, yet the United States bombed and gassed the WACO compound, killing over 80 people including 25 children. While the FRY attempted to deal with an armed terrorist group, the United States and NATO regularly issued threats to use force against the FRY, an act that Western officials referred to as diplomacy backed by force.[43] In spite of FRY cooperation, the threats to use force per-

43 On October 11, Clinton's National Security Advisor, Samuel R. "Sandy" Berger, said that attacks against the FRY could be launched almost immediately. U.S. bombers began landing in Britain as part of a NATO force of 420–430 aircraft preparing for an attack; A-10 Thunderbolts flew from Germany to Italy. The U.S. Defense Secretary threatened that, if NATO went forth with their plans to attack, "there would be a very substantial air campaign that would be capable of inflicting severe damage" (Holley 1998, p. A-6). British Defense Secretary George Robertson said, "If I were Milosevic and I was looking at the B-52 bombers pre-position themselves along with all the other air forces, then I would be very worried and I would be talking unlimitedly with Mr. Holbrooke to get a solution to this" (Holley 1998, p. A6). NATO was illegally threatening force against the FRY while supporting KLA terrorist and separatist activity. On October 12, NATO further ratcheted up the threats by issuing an activation order that brought the NATO allies under the command of NATO supreme commander General Wesley Clark of the United States, deployed NATO military aircraft to Italy, and allowed for a specific package of military air strikes. The order came subsequent to the FRY agreeing to having international observers stationed in Kosovo, withdrawing its troops from the Kosovo province, and accepting a timetable to grant autonomy to Kosovo. Bill Clinton welcomed the moves by FRY authorities but said, "Commitments are not compliance." In addition, UK Prime Minister Tony Blair called the commitments "a breakthrough," but at the same time, he still threatened Belgrade with a military attack, saying NATO was "prepared to use force if necessary" (*BBC News* 13 October 1998). While the ink dried on the agreement between the FRY and the OSCE, U.S. Ambassador to

sisted, actions clearly prohibited by the U.N. Charter: Article 2(4) of the U.N. Charter reads, "All Members shall refrain in their international relations from the *threat* or use of force against the territorial integrity or political independence of any state, or in any other manner inconsistent with the Purposes of the United Nations" (United Nations 2003a, p. 6). Opposition in the Council to the continuing threats by the United States and NATO remained strong, as Russia and China rebuked the threats as detrimental to creating an atmosphere conducive to resolve the issue.[44]

In late October, 1998, the Clinton Administration outsourced the U.S. portion of the Kosovo monitoring contingent to DynCorp,

---

the U.N. Peter Burleigh threatened the use of force again, he said, "The NATO allies, in agreeing on 13 October to the use of force, made it clear that they had the authority, the will and the means to resolve this issue. We retain that authority" (United Nation 1998c, p. 15).

44 Opposition in the Council to continuing threats by NATO was strong. On October 24, Ambassador Lavrov told the Council that NATO should rescind its decision on the option of using force: "We also expect the immediate rescission of the NATO decision on the possible use of force, the so-called activation order, which at present remains in force. This is of particular importance with respect to insuring the safety of OSCE personnel" (United Nations 1998c, p. 12). In addition to being a violation of the U.N. Charter, threatening force is counterproductive for conflict resolution. At the same meeting, Ambassador Qin Huasan of China spoke frankly of his Government's opposition to the continuing threats by NATO to use force against the FRY and the danger posed by such actions: "[V]ery regrettably, almost at the same time as those agreements [between the FRY and parties concerned] were being concluded, a regional organization [NATO] concerned made the decision to take military actions against the Federal Republic of Yugoslavia and interfere in its internal affairs. More disturbingly, that decision was made unilaterally, without consulting the Security Council or seeking its authorization. Such an irresponsible act is not conducive to the creation of a peaceful atmosphere for dealing with the question of Kosovo and will not help resolve the issue. Furthermore, it has violated the purposes, principles, and relevant provisions of the United Nations Charter, as well as international law and widely acknowledged norms governing relations between States. It is a disparagement of and a challenge to the authority of the United Nations and the Security Council and has created an extremely dangerous precedent in international relations. China is gravely concerned about this" (United Nations 1998c, p. 14).

a Virginia based company located close to both the Pentagon and the CIA (Steele 1998, p. 1). Christopher Marquis (2001) writes in the *New York Times* that "the CIA has long been known to set up front companies to mask its activities." Susan Taylor Martin in the *St. Petersburg Times* (Martin 2001, p. 2A) writes that DynCorp is a "major CIA contractor." DynCorp, "an information and aviation giant," would later be "hired" in 2001 by federal officials in Columbia "to conduct drug crop fumigation runs and ferry Columbian troops into conflict zones." Marquis (2001) adds that contracting out work sensitive in nature allows the American military and intelligence agencies to work more discreetly:

> ...in recent years, American military and intelligence agencies have increasingly contracted workers from private companies. The practice allows federal officials to reduce the visibility of sensitive operations by substituting paid civilians for American troops or career intelligence officers.

DynCorp won the bid from the State Department over MPRI, a company that had two previous contracts in the Balkans, one which involved training the Croatian army to conduct "Operation Storm." DynCorp sent about 150 people to Kosovo.

Insiders confirmed that the U.S. was training and supporting the KLA. On January 8, 1999, Dan Everts of the Organization of Security and Cooperation in Europe (OSCE) stated "The north of Albania serves as a training base for the KLA, which is preparing for a war option in the event that political negotiations break down. . . . There is no denying that the north of Albania is a training base for the KLA, which is preparing for battle" (Agence France Presse 1999). A retired U.S. Army Colonel told Fox News that KLA forces were trained at secret bases in Albania by former U.S. military personnel working for MPRI (Madsen 1999). CIA sources disclosed to *The Times* of London that they had trained the KLA:

> American intelligence agents have admitted they helped train the Kosovo Liberation Army before NATO's bombing of Yugoslavia...Central Intelligence officers were ceasefire monitors in Kosovo in 1998 and 1999, developing ties with the KLA and giving American military training manuals and field advice on

fighting the Yugoslav army and Serbian police (Walker & La-verty 2000).

This "disclosure angered some European diplomats," who feared this would make reaching a solution to the conflict more difficult. One European envoy said, "The American agenda consisted of their diplomatic observers, aka the CIA, operating on completely differ-ent terms to the rest of Europe and the OSCE" (Walker & Laverty 2000). A CIA source called the diplomatic observers "a CIA front" (Walker & Laverty 2000). Meanwhile, the KLA boasted that it had "long-standing links" with intelligence agencies on both sides of the Atlantic. Shaban Shala, a KLA commander, stated that as early as 1996, "he had met British, American, and Swiss agents in northern Albania" (Walker & Laverty 2000). In February 2008, Lamberto Dini, former Italian Prime Minister and Foreign Minister and leader of the Italian Liberal Democrats, told the Italian newspaper *Corriere della Sera*, "It was the CIA that provided the Kosovo terrorists and rebels with arms — that is a fact" *(Corriere della Sera* 24 February 2008).

On February 6, 1999, at a chateau in Rambouillet, thirty miles southwest of Paris, the Contact Group (the U.S., U.K., France, Ger-many, Italy, and Russia) hosted talks between the Serbs and the Kosovars, which included the KLA. The first part of the talks lasted 18 days and ended with neither party, the KLA or Belgrade, willing to accept the conditions. The KLA delegation, headed by their Su-preme Commander Hashim Thaci — nicknamed "Snake," wanted a guarantee of Kosovo's independence and not the proposed au-tonomy with a referendum on the future of Kosovo's status after three years.[45] It took 19 days of the United States cajoling the KLA leadership until the Kosovar delegation finally signed, when the talks resumed on March 15. At this time, Albanian State television reported that Ibrahim Rugova, the elected President of Kosovo, had been sentenced to death in absentia by the KLA for signing the Rambouillet Accords (Madsen 1999). Since 1996, the KLA had been

---

45 Thaci would become Kosovo's first president and by 2010 was acknowl-edged as a "big fish" in organized crime and implicated in human organ smuggling.

assassinating moderate Kosovo Albanians to terrify Kosovars into supporting violent insurrection.

The Western media virtually blacked out the Yugoslav proposals at Rambouillet for a peaceful settlement. A number of proposals were put forward, which included the following:

I.   An agreement to stop hostilities in Kosovo and pursue a "peaceful solution through dialogue."

II.   Guaranteed human rights for all citizens, and promotion of the cultural and linguistic identity of each national community.

III.   The facilitated return of all displaced citizens to their homes.

IV.   The widest possible media freedom.

V.   A legislative assembly elected by proportional representation, with additional seats set aside for the various national communities. The assembly's responsibility would include — along with budget and taxes — regulations governing education, environment, medical institutions, urban planning, agriculture, elections, property ownership, and economic, scientific, technological and social development (Parenti 2000, p. 108).

The U.S. and NATO's political proposal was lopsided in favor of the Kosovars, for example, it provided Kosovo with a completely separate judiciary— a Constitution Court and Supreme Court— and an Assembly. Kosovo would also retain guaranteed representation in federal and Serbian governmental institutions, which would not have jurisdiction in Kosovo (*Jurist* 1999). The Serbs finally agreed to the political portion. However, they rejected Appendix B of the accord, which offered them a complete NATO occupation of not only Kosovo but the entire FRY, with unrestricted immunity for any NATO personnel:

> 6b. NATO personnel, under all circumstances and at all times, shall be immune from the Parties' jurisdiction in respect of any civil, administrative, criminal, or disciplinary offenses which may be committed by them in the FRY. The Parties shall assist States participating in the Operation in the exercise of their jurisdiction over their own nationals.

7. NATO personnel shall be immune from any form of arrest, investigation, or detention by the authorities in the FRY. NATO personnel erroneously arrested or detained shall be immediately turned over to NATO authorities.

8. NATO shall enjoy, together with their vehicles, vessels, aircraft, and equipment, free and unrestricted passage and unimpeded access throughout the FRY including associated airspace and territorial waters (U.S. Department of State 1999a, App. B).

Belgrade said it was willing to consider an international peacekeeping force led by a non-military organization such as the OSCE or by the United Nations (*Fairness and Accuracy in Reporting* 14 May 1999). On February 21, 1999, Madeleine Albright appeared on *CNN Late Edition* and the interviewer asked her if the occupying force had to be a NATO force:

Question: "Does it have to be [a] NATO-led force, or as some have suggested, perhaps a U.N.-led force or an OSCE, an Organization of Security and Cooperation in Europe force? Does it specifically have to be NATO run?

Albright: "The United States position is that it has to be a NATO-led force. That is the basis of our participation in it" (U.S. Department of State 1999b).

On the same day, February 21, Madeleine Albright was asked whether she felt the Serbs were acting cooperatively at the talks:

Question: Madame Secretary, what are your feelings about how cooperative is the Serbian side?

Albright: The Serbian side is not cooperative. The Serbian side believes that it can have half the deal, which is to talk about the political part of the document. There are not two documents, there is one document with two parts to it, and one part of it is the political part and another part are [sic] the military and police aspects to it. And there is no deal and no cooperation if they are not willing to engage on what is a basic aspect of the agreement (U.S. Department of State 1999c).

The U.S. and NATO governments labeled Belgrade as uncooperative but were unwilling to accept the slightest compromise to internationalize an occupation force through the U.N. and demanded the Serbs accept an unreasonable ultimatum. Appendix B of the Rambouillet Agreement, the section which the Serbs reject-ed, would have been turned down by any other sovereign nation. Washington and NATO created an image that the Serbs had been offered a peaceful solution, knowing that the FRY, or any other country, could not accept an ultimatum as contained in Appendix B. When the Serbs rejected the stipulations, the U.S. and NATO labeled it "intransigence."

The Western press, the U.S., and NATO governments portrayed Milosevic as someone "digging in his heels" and unwilling to nego-tiate. They had long decided that the Serbs were to be demonized and to be blamed for the chaos and violent conflict in the region, irrespective of the reality that Washington and some of its allies had been financing and training terrorist activities during attempts at a peace settlement. On March 19, 1999, a few days before NATO began bombing the FRY, U.S. State Department Media Briefing Of-ficer James B. Foley commented on the likelihood of war:

> The critical factor here is...whether President Milosevic re-verses course. We are seeing quite the opposite. He's digging in his heels; he's refusing to negotiate. He's putting himself in a position where he will bear the consequences of his obstinacy (Lynch & McGoldrick 2005, p. 101).

The often used rationale of self-defense was not plausible for the United States and NATO because of the internal nature of the con-flict. Hence they turned to a humanitarian justification to rational-ize aggression. Madeleine Albright (2006, p. 61) candidly describes the alternative norm justification that was ruled out in favor of a "humanitarian intervention":

> Since the province was part of Serbia, Milosevic's crimes could not be characterized as international aggression. No member of NATO was under attack, so the alliance could not claim the right of self-defense. Serbia had not threatened to invade anoth-er country, so there was no rationale for a preventative strike. We did, however, have a duty to "defend the vulnerable other."

True humanitarian activists might have noted at the time that a bombing campaign is the least effective tactic for a population suf-fering through a humanitarian crisis. In 2005, revelations surfaced that Strobe Talbott, deputy of State under President Clinton, said,

"It is a small wonder NATO ended up on a collision course. It was Yugoslavia's resistance to the broader trends of political and economic reform — not the plight of the Kosovar Albanians — that best explains NATO's war" (Norris 2005, pp. xxii-xxiii). The day after NATO began bombing the FRY, March 25, 1999, Albright stated that the first of four diplomatic goals was "ensuring that the necessity for military action is understood around the world" (U.S. Department State 1999e). The unnecessary military action did far more harm than good and did create a substantial humanitarian crisis where none had previously existed. The massive flow of refugees did not begin until after the bombing commenced. Chomsky (2004, p. 55-56) writes, "there were an estimated 2,000 killed on all sides during the preceding year [1998]. However, the rich Western documentary record reveals no changes of significance until the March 24 bombing began, apart from a slight increase in Serbian atrocities two days earlier, when monitors were withdrawn in anticipation of the NATO attack." The bombing naturally intensified the conflict and the response from the FRY — having to defend itself both from external aggression and a terrorist separatist movement funded by foreign sources The Serbs not only had to contend with NATO bombardment and the KLA but with dubious foreign fighters. Pilger (2007, p. 278) writes, "During NATO's assault on Serbia in 1999, al-Qaeda militants joined up and fought alongside the Kosovo Liberation Army (KLA)." Under brutal assault from NATO and KLA terrorist strikes, Belgrade responded with force which led to atrocities committed by Serbian forces.

One of the propaganda tools Washington and its allies used was grossly inflating causality figures. While the bombs fell on the FRY, the U.S. Defense Secretary William Cohen said that 100,000 Albanian men "may have been murdered," while David Sheffer, the U.S. envoy for war crimes, said there were as many as 225,000 victims, and Geoff Hoon, at the British Home Office, said there were "at least 10,000" victims — the lowest figure provided by a NATO country (Chandler 2002, p. 73). The preliminary conclusion of the ICTY was that the final death toll of the civil conflict would be between 2,000 and 3,000 people (Chandler 2002, p. 73). The Independent International Commission on Kosovo, in its report, cited official sources, to estimate the number of causalities in Kosovo from February 1998 to March 1999. From February to August 1998, casualty numbers totaled 1050 on both sides, including the KLA. The Commission reported that it is fair to say that the number of killed was much lower during the presence of the KVM monitors from fall 1998 to March 1999:

> The UNHCR reported that 300 people were killed between February and May 1998, and the Council for Defense of Human Rights and Freedoms asserts that 750 people were killed between May and August 1998. But neither set of numbers indicates how many of the victims were KLA members and how many were civilians....it is reasonable to assume that the number of civilian killings was significantly lower during the presence of KVM monitors than during the earlier months (Independent International Commission on Kosovo 2000).

During the U.S.-NATO attack, American officials and media personalities repeated comparisons of Milosevic to Hitler. Executive Director of the Institute for Public Accuracy Norman Solomon (2005, p. 66) writes, "Media database searches attest to how well top Clinton administration officials and like-minded advocates stayed on message about similarities between Hitler and Milosevic." Comparisons to Hitler are passed off as news and become ingrained in the psyche of the population. Solomon adds (2005, p. 66), "Hundreds of times, major media pieces addressed the matter, often in the form of news stories that reported such comparisons by officials without offering a critical counterview." When parallels to Hitler were refuted as inaccurate or as ridiculous, the constant saturation of the Hitler-Milosevic correlation in the mainstream news drowned out these voices of reason. However, this tactic is nothing new. Washington and a subservient mass media have used the Hitler analogy before to demonize foreign leaders and to garner support for the use of force or punitive action. The objects of these attacks include both tyrannical governments that were once supported by the United States and fell out of favor such as Saddam Hussein's regime in Baghdad and governments that were widely popular with their own people and others around the world, such as the Sandinistas in Nicaragua.[46] The Hitler comparisons have been used as propaganda to link an illegal or illegitimate action to World War II and the Holocaust in order to create a perception that military action is necessary to avoid similar horror.

On March 24, 1999, NATO unleashed massive air strikes against the FRY. On that day, the Security Council convened for an emergency meeting and the Rambouillet negotiations were referred to on both sides. NATO governments echoed a uniform position, putting the blame for the conflict on Belgrade while excusing the KLA from responsibility for its terrorist and separatist actions. Other governments, representing the majority of the world's population, including Russia, China, India, and many non-NATO countries expressed outrage. Mr. Lavrov (Russia) stated that a political solution was possible and the diplomacy had not run its course:

> NATO's decision to use military force is particularly unacceptable from any point of view because the potential of political and diplomatic methods to yield a settlement in Kosovo has certainly not been exhausted (United Nations 1999, p. 3).

Not only did diplomacy not run its course, the United States and NATO governments did not attempt a genuine diplomatic solution or negotiation. British politician Lord Gilbert would later state in a

---

46 The Sandinistas were hailed by the World Bank, Oxfam, and other aid agencies as instituting some of the finest poverty relief programs in the early eighties, but the United States viewed the Sandinistas as detrimental to U.S. business interests in Nicaragua, and, therefore, illegally armed and supported the far-right Honduras-based Contras with money filtered from Iran, and initiated a U.S. covert terrorist war. On February 15, 1984, U.S. Secretary of State George Shultz, speaking at the World Affairs Council in Boston, said, "I've had good friends who experienced Germany in the 1930s go there and come back and say, 'I've visited many communist countries, but Nicaragua doesn't feel like that. It feels like Nazi Germany'" (Solomon 2005, p.64). Two weeks after Shultz made these comments, John Silber, the President of Boston University and a Reagan-appointed member of the Bipartisan Commission on Central America, linked Nazi Germany to Nicaragua. Norman Solomon writes that Silber "likened Nicaragua's 'overt' violence to Nazi Germany, without mention that the U.S. government was subsidizing most of the violence in Nicaragua with aid to the Contra guerilla army" (Solomon 2005, p. 64).

2000 U.K. House Inquiry, "I think certain people were spoiling for a fight in NATO at that time. If you ask my personal view, I think the terms put to Milosevic were absolutely intolerable; how could he accept them; it was quite deliberate" (Select Committee on Defence 2000). George Kenney, a former State Department Yugoslavia desk officer writes that "[a]n unimpeachable source who regularly travels with Secretary of State Madeleine Albright" witnessed "a senior State Department official brag that the United States 'deliberately set the bar higher than the Serbs could accept'" (*Fairness and Accuracy in Reporting* 2 Jun. 1999). Jim Jatras, a foreign policy aide to Senate Republicans, confirmed Kenney's description, stating that he had it "on good account" that a "senior administration official told media at Rambouillet, under embargo" the following: "We intentionally set the bar too high for the Serbs to comply. They need some bombing, and that's what they are going to get" (*Fairness and Accuracy in Reporting* 2 Jun. 1999).

The NATO air campaign against the FRY, "Operation Allied Force," lasted 78 days, from March 24 until June 10, and was waged under the pretext of humanitarian intervention. NATO aircraft flew more than 38,000 sorties and dropped 23,000 bombs on the FRY (*PBS.org* 2008; U.S. Department of Defense 1999). FRY authorities claimed that NATO had killed at least 1,200 and as many as 5,000 civilians with its bombing campaign. Human Rights Watch reported that at least 500 civilians were killed. HRW officials visited ninety-one cities, towns, and villages and concluded that "NATO committed violations of international humanitarian law" and the organization called on NATO governments "to establish an independent and *impartial* commission to investigate these violations and issue its findings publicly" (Human Rights Watch 2000). NATO also dropped cluster bombs, which are banned under international law. According to the HRW, by May 13, when the United States stopped dropping cluster bombs, up to 150 civilians had been killed by the illegal munitions. The United Kingdom continued to use cluster bombs until the end of the bombing campaign. HRW documented NATO's targeting of many non-military sites, including "the headquarters of Serb Radio and Television in Belgrade, the

New Belgrade heating plant, and seven bridges that were neither major transportation routes nor had other military functions" (Human Rights Watch 2000). Many other incidents were officially documented including the targeting of convoys, a weather station, and a sanatorium (Human Rights Watch 2000). The United States also bombed the Chinese Embassy in Belgrade. The United States and NATO claimed it was an accident, but others argued that the embassy was targeted because of China's strong opposition to NATO's use of force against the FRY.

On June 15, German NATO troops supervised the mass exodus of terrified Serbs being ethnically cleansed from the southeastern town of Prizren. The *Evening Standard* of London reported that the German troops were apparently "powerless to stop it" (Stephen 1999, p. 4). The persecuted Serbs "packing possessions into cars, vans and trucks, poured on to the street in a great convoy" (Stephen 1999, p. 4). The Serbian news agency Beta Vitria reported on July 21 that twelve villages in Southeastern Kosovo were "cleansed" of Serbs *(Beta News Agency* 21 Jul. 1999). Amidst the persecution, Kosovar Albanians burnt Orthodox churches to the ground, destroying centuries of history and artifacts. In 2004, the Serbian Orthodox Church filed a lawsuit against the United Kingdom, France, Italy, and Germany for failing to protect Orthodox churches in Kosovo. Bishop Artemije of Raska and Prizren said that eighty churches were destroyed by fire from 1999 to 2004. In addition, monasteries, frescos, and medieval icons were targeted and destroyed (*BBC News* 9 Dec. 2004). On December 6, 1999, the OSCE released a three-hundred-page report documenting "a campaign of persecution and racist murders by Kosovars against Serbs and all other non-Albanians since June 1999 when NATO took control (Renton 1999, p. 6). The *Evening Standard* of London said, "The 300-page report lists in methodical, gruesome detail thousands of crimes — from the murder of bedridden old women to the intimidation of other Muslims just because they speak Serbo-Croat — committed in Kosovo in the last five months" (Renton 1999, p. 6). The report did not give casualty totals but specifically details "well over 100 murders of Serbs" (Renton 1999, p. 6).

In 2001, the KLA conveniently changed its name to the NLA (National Liberation Army) and invaded its sovereign neighbor, Macedonia. James Bissett, former Canadian ambassador to Yugoslavia, Bulgaria, and Albania from 1990-1992, charged that NATO was responsible for the KLA's aggression in Macedonia:

> NATO allowed the KLA, which under the terms of the United Nations Resolution 1244 was to be disarmed after the end of the bombing, to keep its weapons. The KLA was renamed the Kosovo Protection Force and had been given the task of maintaining peace and security in Kosovo. How well it has been able to carry out this task is summed up in a report dated Feb. 26, 2001, to the Secretary General of the United Nations, Kofi Annan, which accuses the protection corps of widespread acts of murder, torture, and extortion (Bissett 2001).

In March 2001, the Secretary General of NATO, Lord Robertson, blasted the terrorist activities of the KLA, calling the KLA "murderous thugs" (Bissett 2001). However, the United States had a different policy path. Robert Fenwick, the head of the OSCE in Europe, secretly met with leaders of the KLA and Albanian political parties, but Macedonian officials were not given any invitation. Bissett writes that it was clear that the U.S. was backing the KLA's aggression:

> This was confirmed a month later, when a force of 400 KLA fighters was surrounded in the town of Aracinovo near the capital, Skopje. As Macedonian security forces moved in, they were halted on NATO orders. U.S. army buses from Camp Bondsteel in Kosovo arrived to remove all the heavy armed terrorists to a safer area of Macedonia. German reporters later revealed that 17 U.S. military advisers were accompanying the KLA terrorists in Aracinovo. In August, fearing the Macedonian forces might be able to defeat the KLA, the U.S. Security Advisor flew to Kiev and ordered the Ukrainian government to stop sending further military equipment to Macedonia (Bissett 2001).

The KLA took control of nearly thirty percent of the Macedonian territory. Goran Stevanovic, a sergeant with an elite Macedonian police unit, said, "If NATO hadn't been arming and equipping the UCK [KLA] in Kosovo there would be no need for them to 'disarm' these guerillas now in Macedonia" (Taylor 2001).

The U.S.-NATO argument that war against the FRY was for humanitarian purposes is illogical when one examines their behavior and the consequences of their actions. The Kosovo situation had a political, diplomatic and peaceful solution. Initially, external influences fueled the conflict. Then external military aggression created a humanitarian nightmare. However, humanitarian intervention was merely the alternative norm justification used by the U.S. and NATO governments to create a perception of legitimacy.

The Independent International Commission on Kosovo was partially correct in its analysis: the 1999 NATO attack on the FRY was illegal. The report was incorrect to state that the attack was legitimate. There is no way to avoid the black and white of the law and that NATO bypassed the Security Council and unilaterally attacked the FRY. However, legitimacy is a more complicated concept; it is an idea that can be both real and falsely perceived. Rulers and their governments have used the Weberian philosophy of legitimacy by conducting intense public relations and media campaigns to produce a false perception of legitimacy.

The Independent International Commission on Kosovo could not escape the clear fact of the illegality of NATO's actions against the FRY; however, the Commission attempted to propagandize and create a perception of legitimacy by concluding that NATO's attack was "illegal but legitimate." The Commission was established for NATO public relations and for damage control against criticism. On August 6, 1999, Swedish Prime Minister Göran Persson, announced the creation of the Commission. Sweden is not a member of NATO but, since 1994, has been a member of the Partnership for Peace (PfP) with NATO and has traditionally been a partner to the Western alliance. Despite its official neutrality during the Cold War, Sweden regularly collaborated with NATO. By having the Swedish Prime Minister announce the Commission, it would create a perception that the Commission was neutral. The Swedish government was only directly involved in the Commission through their "invitation to Justice Richard Gladstone of South Africa and to Mr. Carl Tham of the Olof Palme International Center in Stockholm to act as chairman and co-chairman respectively" (Independent International Commission on Kosovo 2000). The additional eleven members of the Commission were made after invitations were extended by Justice Gladstone and Mr. Tham:

> Dr. Hanan Ashwari (Palestine), Professor Grace d'Almeida (Benin), Senator Akiko Domoto (Japan), Professor Richard Falk (United States), Ambassador Oleg Grinevsky (Russian Federation), Mr. Michael Ignatieff (Canada), Professor Mary Kaldor (United Kingdom), Professor Martha Minow (United States), Professor Jacques Rupnik (France), Theo Sommer (Germany), and Jan Urban (Czech Republic) (Independent International Commission on Kosovo 2000).

The first obvious fact when looking at the Commission's appointed members is that seven out of eleven members are from NATO countries. The name Independent International Commission on Kosovo was chosen because it sounds official and neutral, but instead, the Commission was partial to helping the reputation of the Western powers that were participating in the aggression against the FRY. The report was not a United Nations report, but the Commission attempted to benefit from U.N. legitimacy by saying that the plan was "informally discussed" with Kofi Annan who "endorsed the project" (Independent International Commission on Kosovo 2000). In the Commission's Mission Statement, the phrase "the role of the United Nations and NATO's decision to intervene militarily" is intended to mislead and create a connection between the United Nations and NATO's intervention. The research in the report covers many facets to the conflict, but the conclusion that NATO's intervention was "illegal but legitimate" was incorrect. While the body of the report contained reasonable reportage, the conclusion, which is what is most often read and referred to, is an example of an attempt to create a Weberian perception of legitimacy.

Humanitarian Rhetoric and Hypocrisy

Even the worst aggressor states in world history have offered justifications for waging war. In 1949, the International Court of Justice (ICJ) concluded that the use of force to intervene in the name of international justice "has, in the past, given rise to most serious abuses" (Franck & Rodley 1973, p. 302). In 1973, Franck and Rodley published a study in the *American Journal of International Law* in which they examined the history of states using the justification of "humanitarian intervention" for the use of force in another country. They concluded that, "in very few, if any, instances has the right [to humanitarian intervention] been asserted under the circumstances that appear more humanitarian than self-seeking and power seeking" (Franck & Rodley 1973, p. 290).

In 1999, The United States Senate voted 58 to 41 in favor of using military force against the Federal Republic of Yugoslavia (FRY). On March 23, a day before the bombing began, CNN's Larry King told Madeleine Albright that Senator Pete Domenici, who voted to oppose authorizing military force, had stated, "We don't have an obligation to send our men and women of the military in every time there's a humanitarian problem in this world or a civil strife or a revolution." King asked Albright, "What would you say to him?" Albright responded, "Well. We don't; the truth is that we don't send them in every time. But when we think that our national interests have been affected and could be affected in a much worse way, then I believe it's a smart thing to do" (U.S. Department of State 1999d). The same year NATO attacked the FRY, the world watched while Indonesian forces massacred the people of East Timor and chased them from their homes. Human Rights Watch describes the horrors of September 1999:

> The world watched in horror in September 1999 when the Indonesian National Army (TNI) and Timorese militias went on a campaign of murder, arson, and forced expulsion after the people of East Timor voted for independence in a United Nations administered referendum. After almost twenty-five years of brutal occupation, an estimated 1,000 to 2,000 East Timorese civilians lost their lives in the months before, and days immediately after, the voting. Approximately 500,000 people were forced from their homes or fled to seek refuge" (Human Rights Watch 2006).

The mass killings of the East Timor people included the unspeakable massacres of clergy and refugees seeking shelter in a church. Women, children, and Jesuit priests were killed. The *Sydney Morning Herald* reported, "The blood was that of women, children, and priests massacred at the church by pro-Indonesian militias last Monday" (Widyastuty 13 Sept. 1999, p. 8). Some Western countries not only watched but indirectly participated in the massacres by arming and training the Indonesia military and its subsidiaries. *The Guardian* of London reported on September 19, 1999, "Indonesian military forces linked to the carnage in East Timor were trained in the United States under a covert programme sponsored by the Clinton Administration which continued until last year" (Vulliamy & Barnett 1999). The U.S. program, concealed from lawmakers, was codenamed "Iron Balance." The same report disclosed details on the UK and U.S. training projects:

> The Observer can also disclose that the Government [UK] has spent about one million British pounds in training more than 50 members of the Indonesian military in Britain since it came to power. Pentagon documents revealed a secret training program under a project called JCET (Joint Combined Education and Training). ... [T]he training [U.S.] was in military expertise that could be used internally against civilians, such as urban guerilla warfare, surveillance, counter-intelligence, sniper marksmanship and "psychological operation," ... since May 1997, 24 senior members of Indonesia's forces have been trained in U.K. military colleges (Vulliamy & Barnett 1999).

The U.S. and NATO attacked the FRY even though a tangible diplomatic and political solution existed. Not only did NATO attack, but several NATO countries were directly involved in inflaming the conflict through their covert arming and training of the KLA. The propaganda war against the FRY put forth a case that Milosevic was driven by ethnic hatred and that no alternative to the use of force existed. The same year, East Timorese people were massacred for daring to cast a ballot in a United Nations referendum.

There exist numerous examples of hypocritical human rights rhetoric. Turkey, a NATO member, is a country with widely documented human rights abuses. Douglas Bandow, senior fellow at the CATO institute, says that in the face of Turkey's abominable human rights record and repression of Kurds and Cypriots, "NATO, despite its supposed commitment to humanitarian values, does nothing. The Clinton administration voices no outrage, proposes no bombing of Ankara, demands no NATO occupation to restore the rights of beleaguered Kurds and Greek Cypriots" (Bandow 2000, p. 37). The domestic human rights record of the Turkish state remains very serious:

> The army suppresses parties and dictates policy. Moreover, according to Human Rights Watch, "Police continue to shoot and kill peaceful demonstrators" To advocate education in the Kurdish language is to risk jail. Supporters of Kurdish autonomy face trial for treason. In March 1999, the U.S.-based Committee to Protect Journalists announced that "for the fifth consecutive year, Turkey had more journalists in prison than any other country." Most of them "are victims of the government's continued criminalization of reporting" on the conflict in Kurdistan. All told, reports Human Rights Watch, there is "massive continuing abuse of human rights in Turkey" (Bandow 2000, p. 36).

Many examples of double standards and hypocrisy exist in Western human rights rhetoric. The NATO intervention in Kosovo was particularly striking because NATO appealed for Belgrade to respect the same norms that the alliance was in the process of breaking. On April 12, during NATO's "Operation Allied Force," the alliance issued a press statement explaining NATO's goals for the operation. Point four of this statement indicates that the FRY will continue to be attacked unless it respects international law and the United Nations Charter:

> NATO's air strikes will be pursued until President Milosevic accedes to the demands of the international community. President Milosevic knows what he has to do. He must . . . provide credible assurance of his willingness to work on the basis of the Rambouillet Accords in the establishment of a political framework agreement for Kosovo in conformity with international law and the United Nations Charter (NATO 1999).

The glaring hypocrisy is evident. In this statement, NATO arrogantly represents itself as the spokesperson for the international community, despite having bypassed the only legitimate organization representing the international community, the United Nations. It is a demonstration of the unique universal legitimacy of the

United Nations Charter, when even an entity in the process of violating the Charter refers to it as an objective standard of legitimacy.

CHAPTER EIGHT: A PATH TOWARD PEACE AND SECURITY

The greatest violators of the U.N. Charter are the United States and its NATO allies. To be sure, less powerful states have violated the Charter by employing the unilateral use of force, yet states that are not strongly allied to a permanent member are usually condemned or, at the very least, judged according to the criteria of the U.N. Charter and international law. At times weaker nations are judged unfairly and blamed for actions for which they are not responsible, and in that case, weaker states rarely have the tools or prestige to counter the charges of the powerful accusing state or states. Permanent members of the Security Council have frequently been given a pass before international law and the Charter because of their veto privilege, their power, and their public relations machinery. The most powerful governments, especially the United States, have waged public relations campaigns to justify aggression and in the process have distorted international law to fit their actions.

U.N. reform proposals put forth by groups, such as the G-4 or the African Group, are attempting to change the make-up of the Security Council by enlarging it and making it more representative of the world in the 21st Century. Democratizing and diversifying the Council is certainly a positive step toward modernizing and perhaps strengthening the United Nations, still the veto privilege makes substantive reform difficult. Permanent members have little incentive to share with other countries the privileges they currently enjoy. Nevertheless, if substantive reform on Security Council expansion is achieved, it will accomplish little toward strengthening the Security Council, the United Nations, and international law, as long as powerful permanent members continue to violate international norms and the U.N. Charter without being held accountable for their illegal and illegitimate actions.

A serious reform agenda must involve addressing the abuses by the most powerful permanent member states, because they remain the most likely to commit illegal and illegitimate actions with impunity. When the U.S. and NATO, a technologically advanced military alliance, attacks a small country, bypassing the authority of the U.N. Security Council, and constructing its own justifications for aggression, how is it to be held liable? As the previous chapters have demonstrated, powerful countries seek legitimacy when they use force, and if they fail to obtain the legitimacy of the United Nations, they attempt to create the perception of legitimacy using alternative norm justifications, claiming force is necessary for humanitarian reasons or self-defense. Additionally, when actions are taken, legal arguments are made by using ambiguous resolutions or inverted logic; for example, in 1981, the Security Council condemned Israel for unilaterally bombing the Iraqi Osiraq nuclear reactor, and it was absurdly claimed that, because the condemnation was not accompanied by sanctions, it was actually a statement of approval (D'Amato 1983, p. 586).

Powerful countries do care about legitimacy, but it is unrealistic to add an independent judicial body to rule on actions taken by the Council or by its members because substantive changes to the Council and the General Assembly are subject to a permanent-five veto. Positive developments such as the International Criminal Court are subject to boycott and political manipulation by dominant countries. The central strategy toward creating serious reform of holding powerful permanent-member states accountable is to expose the falseness of Weber's definition of legitimacy. In order to better assure that states are held accountable to the rules and regulations of the U.N. Charter and international law, two areas must become a focus of U.N. reform, media and education.

Eliminating Weber's Definition of Legitimacy

Max Weber has contributed overwhelmingly to the social sciences; however, his definition of legitimacy must be eliminated from the social sciences. In their quest for empirical evidence, social scientists have used Weber's definition to measure legitimacy instead of applying objective standards. Uphoff (1989, p.312) writes, "[L] egitimacy is produced by members of the public to the extent that they believe, and are willing to act on their belief, that specific exercises of authority are right and proper, deserving to be obeyed." This conception of legitimacy has been, as Beetham (1991, p. 8) writes, "an almost unqualified disaster." Stillman (1974, p. 39) writes, "The definition of legitimacy should be re-examined, because the current social science definitions are in practice not pervasive and in theory weak, containing apparently unconscious and concealed arbitrariness." Stillman (1974, p. 50) notes that in a Friedrich-like definition [Weberian definition], "a charismatic leader beloved by most of his people for his style and rhetoric , who leads his country to national destruction — a Hitler — is legitimate if legitimacy be defined in terms of popular attitudes." Stillman (1974, p. 50) continues by addressing the problem with social scientists accepting that a belief in legitimacy is legitimacy; he writes, "Furthermore, if only popular attitudes matter, then in effect that government is most legitimate which propagandizes most effectively, which socializes most efficiently, which manipulates public opinion best." NATO actions in the former Yugoslavia, conducted without Security Council approval, relied on manipulating public opinion to create a perception of legitimacy. Other examples covered in the preceding chapters — for example the Grenada, Iraq, Afghanistan, and Panama interventions — used the same conception of legitimacy. Weber's definition of legitimacy must be discarded, because it is false. Also, it is a tool for the most powerful to manipulate public opinion.

The U.N. Charter, the supreme international treaty, has been formally agreed to by 194 member states. International law is enshrined in the UN Charter and other relevant treaties, as well as customary law. States, as signatories to the Charter, have universally expressed consent and shared beliefs for the U.N. and that consent continues to be communicated through various forms of active compliance. All countries, large and small, agreed to give the Security Council the primary responsibility for the maintenance of international peace and security while upholding the Charter. Permanent members of the Security Council hold the most responsibility when addressing breaches of international peace and security. It was through the consent and shared beliefs of the international community and the codification of U.N. law that the Security Council became legitimate. It is the corporate identity of the Security Council that retains this legitimacy, and when individual permanent members breach international norms and the U.N. Charter by using unilateral force, they do so illegitimately without the consent and shared beliefs of the international community and without the backing of international law.

By understanding the formula for legitimacy and how propaganda is used to create the perception of legitimacy, people are better equipped to oppose and fight against illegitimate uses of power that most often lead to increased human suffering and tragedy. Weberian defined legitimacy has been used as a tool by governments to influence the public's perception of what is legitimate; the public is left watching shadows on the wall while only a few make their way from the cave, as in Plato's *The Republic* (Plato 1992, pp. 197-200). Beetham's formula for legitimacy allows ordinary people to give power structures guidelines in order to act within a legitimate framework. This objective framework must replace the current preference for Weber's definition of legitimacy among academics in the social sciences.

Media Reform

Today's mass media all but universally disseminate information in the interests of the country to which they belong. Thus, in a conflict situation, with concrete facts on the ground, two different media outlets, representing each country's party to the conflict, can have fundamentally different analyses of the hostilities. Fox News in the U.S., owned by Rupert Murdoch, is an explicit example of a media outlet promoting a national agenda. Fox not only promotes a national agenda, like the other networks, it promotes a specific right-wing agenda, which is the reason for it being widely criticized. Other American networks remain more neutral in covering the Democratic and Republican parties; however, all major U.S. networks push the agenda of the U.S. political structure. This was seen clearly in the months leading up to the 2003 Iraq invasion, when dissenting voices were marginalized and silenced.

In the United States, C-SPAN channels broadcast regular hearings of the U.S. Congress, as well as other public policy related events. An important step toward serious reform must include the dissemination of U.N. television to the world. U.N. television is currently available via the internet with video footage of Security Council meetings, news, and educational programming. The U.N. and the Charter must begin to enter the consciousness of people to reverse the common acceptance of statements such as the one made by Hillary Clinton while campaigning for President in 2007: "I don't believe it's in the best interests of our country to give the United Nations what amounts to a veto over presidential action" (*MSNBC. com* 27 Sept. 2007). Hillary Clinton is not alone as this is sometimes a widely expressed opinion made by American politicians. In 1996, Bob Dole, in his campaign for President against Bill Clinton, engaged in scare tactics by warning the public that Bill Clinton would hand U.S. sovereignty over to the U.N. In 2004, John Kerry was disparaged at the Republican Convention when Zell Miller, a conservative Democrat, warned that Kerry would cede American power to Paris and the U.N. (MSNBC.com 3 Sept. 2004). In 1970, Kerry had said that force should be used only at the "directive of the United Nations;" however, in his acceptance for the 2004 Democratic nomination, he said, "I will never hesitate to us force when it is required. Any attack will be met with a swift and certain response. I will never give any nation or international institution a veto over our national security" (*Factcheck.org* 4 Oct. 2004). The public needs to be educated and understand the history of the U.N. Charter, and it must be made aware that the United States and every other country must abide by the clear rules and regulations agreed to in the international treaty signed at the San Francisco Conference in 1945.

John Avery (2005) proposed several ideas relating to the establishment of a United Nations television network:

> Why doesn't the United Nations have its own global television and radio network? Such a network could produce an unbiased version of the news. It could broadcast documentary programs on global problems. It could produce programs showing viewers the music, art and literature of other cultures than their own. It could broadcast programs on the history of ideas, in which the contributions of many societies were adequately recognized. At New Year, when people are in the mood to think of the past and the future, the Secretary General of the United Nations could broadcast a "State of the World" message, summarizing the events of the past year and looking forward to the new year, with its problems, and with his recommendations for their solution. A United Nations television and radio network would at least give viewers and listeners a choice between programs supporting militarism, and programs supporting a global culture of peace. At present they have little choice.

A U.N. network must always reinforce the U.N. Charter and its rules and procedures. The network would be run by the U.N. Secretariat, and the network's staff would be comprised of U.N. civil servants from a wide variety of nations from every region of the world. It would represent a truly global network with programming designed to reinforce the unique legality and legitimacy of the U.N. Charter in international affairs. This network is a must to begin addressing the use of perception of legitimacy to justify illegitimate actions by powerful states. Weber's definition can then begin to be challenged by Beetham's formula that sets down objective standards for what makes a legitimate action.

Education

Any serious attempt at reinforcing the U.N. Charter and holding powerful states accountable for gross violations of international law must also begin with a strong campaign to address the lack of education on the United Nations. In the U.S., the history and basic principles of the United Nations are not required curriculum, but are left to the discretion of individual educators. On November 19, 1974, the General Conference of UNESCO (United Nations Educational Scientific and Cultural Organization) adopted the "Recommendations Concerning Education for International Understanding Co-operation and Peace and Education relating to Human Rights and Fundamental Freedoms." The document describes key ingredients for peace education. Item 3.3, the first guiding principle, states that education should promote the work of the United Nations:

> Education should be infused with the aims and purposes set forth in the Charter of the United Nations, the Constitution of UNESCO and the Universal Declaration of Human Rights, particularly Article 26, paragraph 2, of the last-named, which states: "Education shall be directed to the full development of the human personality and to the strengthening of respect for human rights and fundamental freedoms. It shall promote understanding, tolerance and friendship among all nations, racial or religious groups, and shall further the activities of the United Nations for the maintenance of peace (UNESCO 2005, p. 2).

The United Nations and Retaining Control

The ideal of the United Nations Charter is universally respected and is the reason for the continued legitimacy of the organization. However, this legitimacy cannot continuously be abused by the United States and NATO governments. Dag Hammarskjöld, the second U.N. Secretary General, stated, "The principles of the [Charter of the United Nations] are, by far, greater than the organization in which they are embodied, and the aims which they safeguard are holier than the policies of any single nation or people" (Jackson 1957, p. 431).

It is imperative that the United Nations retains any and all command and control over the authorization of the use of force. To allow the United States or NATO to enforce a U.N. resolution with military force only results in Washington abusing the mandate and using it for an expanded agenda. This was the case in spring 2011 when the United Nations authorized 'no-fly zones' over Libya. The United States, France, and Britain, used the Security Council resolution to punish Libya with a bombing campaign, including Tripoli, with an agenda not to protect but to carry out regime change.

Long-Term Western Interests

The international community continues to legitimize the United Nations, specifically the Security Council, on both the intergovernmental level and the domestic level. The United Nations is a check on national power, and it provides a clear set of rules and regulations to follow based on internationally agreed upon norms and laws.

It remains in the long-term strategic interests of the United States and Western powers to adhere to and promote objective norms and regulations governing international relations. The 21st century promises that the United States will no longer be the hegemonic power of the immediate post-Cold War era. The first decade of the 21st century has already witnessed the rapid rise of China as a global economic power and the resurgence of a powerful Russia. India also continues to grow at a rapid pace. If Western countries choose to continue to violate the norms governing the international system, they will have set a dangerous precedent for how the future superpower or powers will be allowed to conduct their international policy. Therefore, it is in their own strategic self-interest to change from the current dominant Weberian approach to legitimacy to Beetham's objective formula: legality, consent from subordinate actors, and shared beliefs between dominant and subordinate. This formula is enshrined in the U.N. Charter. The United Nations holds the unique universal legitimacy found in no other international institution.

ACKNOWLEDGEMENTS

I thank Ambassador André Lewin, former spokesman for the U.N. Secretary General, for his support. I extend my gratitude to the faculty of Centre d'Études Diplomatiques et Stratégiques (CEDS) in Paris for the excellent education and mentorship, and to the Department of Political Science at Stockholm University in Sweden for granting me visiting fellowship status to conduct research for this book. Additionally, I would like to thank the University of Oregon Library, Portland State University Library, and the staff at the Dag Hammarskjöld Library at the University of Uppsala in Sweden. Most importantly, I thank my parents, Karen and Fred Aranas, for their tremendous love and support, who taught me to speak truth to power and to work for justice and peace.

REFERENCES

'Ad spending in presidential race triples that of 2000' 2004, *Minnesota Public Radio*, 01 Nov., viewed on 24 April 2011, ‹http://news.minnesota.publicradio.org/features/2004/11/01_ap_adspending›

Albright, M 2006, '*The mighty and the almighty: reflections on America, God, and world affairs*', Harper Collins, New York.

Almasmari, H 2011, 'U.S. makes a drone attack a day in Yemen', *The National*, 15 Jun, viewed on 30 July 2011, ‹http://www.thenatioal.ae/news/worldwide/middle-east/us--makes-a-drone-attack-a-day-in-yemen›.

Amnesty International 2005, 'Croatia: operation "Storm" –still no justice ten years on (EUR 64/002/2005)', 4 Aug, viewed 26 September 2007, ‹http://www.amnesty.org/fr/library/asset/EUR64/002/2005/fr/dom-EUR640022005en.html›.

Antelava, N 2004, 'US military will stay in Georgia', *BBC News*, 18 Jan, viewed 19 August 2008, ‹http://news.bbc.co.uk/2/hi/europe/3406941.stm›.

Apple, RW Jr. 1990, 'Mideast tensions: the barriers facing bush; Gulf actions expose foreign policy limits', *New York Times*, 14 Nov, p. A1.

Arend, AC 2003, 'International law and the preemptive use of military force', *The Washington Quarterly*, vol. 26, no. 2, pp. 89-103.

Atkinson, R & Gellman, B 1991, 'Iraq trying to shelter jets in Iran, U.S. says; Saddam says much blood will be shed', *Washington Post*, 29 Jan, p. A1.

Avery, J 2005, 'Learning to live in harmony', *H.C. Ørsted Institute*, 18 Aug, viewed 4 January 2009, ‹http://www.learndev.org/dl/harmony8.pdf›.

Baker, JA III 1995, *The politics of diplomacy*, Putnam, New York.

Baldwin, DA 2002, 'Power and international relations', in W Carlsnaes, T Risse & BA Simmons (eds.), *Handbook of International Relations*, Sage, London.

Bandow, D 2000, 'NATO's hypocritical humanitarianism', in TG Carpenter (ed.), *NATO's empty victory: a postmortem on the Balkan War*, Cato Institute, Washington, DC.

Barratt-Brown, M 2005, *From Tito to Milosevic: Yugoslavia, the lost country*, Merlin Press, London.

Bauder, D 2008, 'CNN reporter talks of pressure to be patriotic', *Associated Press*, 29 May, viewed 1 October 2008, <http://abcnews.go.com/Entertainment/WireStory?id=4959585&page=1>.

Beckman, O 2005, *Armed intervention: pursuing legitimacy and the pragmatic use of legal argument*, Ph.D., Lund University, Lund.

Beetham, D 1991, *The legitimation of power*, Humanities Press International, Atlantic Highlands, NJ.

Beitzell, R (ed) 1970, *Tehran, Yalta, Potsdam: the Soviet protocols*, Academic International, Hattiesburg, MS.

'Belgrade daily comments on Croatia's "ongoing speedy arming"', 1993, *Yugoslav Telegraph Service news agency*, as provided by BBC Summary of World Broadcasts, 16 Nov, EE/1849/C, viewed 16 July 2008, LexisNexis Academic Universe.

Bennett, C 1995, *Yugoslavia's bloody collapse: causes, course, and consequences*, Hurst, London.

Bhatta, G 2000, *Reforms at the United Nations: contextualising the Annan agenda*, Singapore University Press, Singapore.

Biden, JR Jr. 1995, 'Statement of Joseph R. Biden on lifting the arms embargo on Bosnia', *CQ (Congressional Quarterly)*, press release, 26 July.

Bissett, J 2001, 'War on terrorism skipped the KLA', *National Post/Centre for Research on Globalization (CRG)* 23 November, viewed 23 September 2008, <http://globalresearch.ca/articles/BIS11A.html>.

Bonner, R & Weiner, T 1996, 'Gun-running in the Balkans: CIA and diplomats collide', *New York Times*, 29 May, p. A1.

Bookman, M 1994, War and Peace: The Divergent Breakups of Yugoslavia and Czechoslovakia, *Journal of Peace Research*, vol. 31, pp. 175-187.

Borger, J 2006, 'US campaign to stop Venezuela joining UN security council', *The Guardian*, 20 June, viewed 10 September 2007, <http://www.guardian.co.uk/world/2006/jun/20/venezuela.usa>.

Borger, J & Wilson, J 2005, 'US 'backed by illegal Iraqi oil deals', *The Guardian*, 16 May, viewed 15 September 2011, <http:www.guardian.co.uk/world/2005/may/17/otherparties.iraq>.

Bortin, M 2007, 'U.S. faces more distrust from world, poll shows', *New York Times*, 28 Jun, p. A12.

Boutros-Ghali, B 1999, *Unvanquished: a U.S.-U.N. saga*, Random House, New York.

Boyd, CG 1995, 'Making peace with the guilty; the truth about Bosnia', *Foreign Affairs*, Sep/Oct, vol. 74, no. 5, p. 22.

Boyes, R & Wright, E 1999, 'Drugs money linked to Kosovo rebels', *The Times (London)*, 24 Mar, viewed 2 January 2009, LexisNexis Academic Universe.

Broughel, T & Rendall, S 2003, 'Amplifying officials, squelching dissent: FAIR study finds democracy poorly served by war coverage', *Fairness and Accuracy in Reporting FAIR*, May/June, viewed 13 November 2007, ‹http://www.fair.org/index.php?page=1145›.

Brubaker, B 2006, 'Panama wins U.N. Security Council seat', *Washington Post*, 7 Nov, viewed 10 September 2007, ‹http://from www.washingtonpost.com›.

Bureau of International Organization Affairs 2005, 'Voting practice in the United Nations, 2004: report to Congress submitted pursuant to public laws 101-246 and 108-447', Bureau of International Organization Affairs, Washington D.C.

'Bush meets with Yugoslav prime minister' 1989, *Associated Press*, 13 Oct.

Butler, R 2000, *Saddam defiant: the threat of weapons of mass destruction and the crisis of global security*, Wiedenfeld & Nicolson, London.

Carpenter, TG 2000, 'Damage to relations with Russia and China', in TG Carpenter (ed.), *NATO's empty victory: a postmortem on the Balkan War*, Cato Institute, Washington, DC.

Central Intelligence Agency 2005, 'Memorandum for the record 9/29/98 (C/98-06145), approved for release September 2005', Freedom of Information Act (FOIA), Central Intelligence Agency, Langley.

Chandler, D 2002, *From Kosovo to Kabul: human rights and international intervention*, Pluto Press, London.

Chapman, TL & Reiter, D 2004, 'The United Nations Security Council and the rally 'round the flag effect', *Journal of Conflict Resolution* vol. 48, no. 6, pp. 886-909.

Chayes, A & Chayes, AH 1995, *The new sovereignty: compliance with international regulatory agreements*, Harvard University Press, Cambridge.

Chivers, CJ & Barry, E 2008, 'Accounts undercut claims by Georgia on Russia war', *New York Times*, 7 Nov, p. A1.

Chomsky, N 2000, *Rogue states: the rule of force in world affairs*, South End Press, Cambridge.

Chomsky, N 2004, *Hegemony or survival: America's quest for global dominance*, Penguin Books, New York

Chossudovsky, M 1996, 'Dismantling Yugoslavia colonizing Bosnia', *Covert Action Quarterly*, Spring, no. 56.

Chossudovsky, M 1997, *The globalisation of poverty: impacts of IMF and World Bank reforms*, Third World Network, Penang.

'CIA gave Kosovo "terrorists" weapons – Italian politician' 2008, *Corriere della Sera*, originally in Italian, as provided by BBC Monitoring Europe - Political, 24 Feb, viewed 27 June 2008, LexisNexis Academic Universe.

Clark, WK 2001, *Waging modern war: Bosnia, Kosovo, and the future of combat*, Public Affairs, New York.

Clemens, DS 1970, *Yalta*, Oxford University Press, Oxford.

Cohen, R 1993, 'U.S. allies differ on arms for Bosnian Muslims', *New York Times*, 22 Apr, p. A15.

Crandall, R 2006, *Gunboat democracy: U.S. interventions in the Dominican Republic, Grenada, and Panama*, Rowman and Littlefield, Oxford.

Crossette, B 1997, The world; for Iraq, a dog house with many rooms', *New York Times*, 23 Nov, viewed 15 September 2011, <http://www.nytimes.com/1997/11/23/weekinreview/the-world-for-iraq-a-dog-house-with-many-rooms.html>.

Crossette, B 1998, 'Standoff with Iraq: the highlights; accord is reported to open eight Iraqi sites', *New York Times*, 23 Feb, p. A8.

D'Amato, A 1983, 'Israel's air strike upon the Iraqi Nuclear Reactor', *American Journal of International Law*, vol. 77, no. 3, pp. 584-588.

Dole, B 1990, 'Don't turn Yugoslavia into Europe's Lebanon; uneven progress', *New York Times*, 3 Dec, Sec. A, p. 18.

Domarus, M 1997, *Hitler speeches and proclamations 1932-1945: the chronicle of a dictatorship volume three the years 1939 to 1940*, Bolchazy-Carducci, Wauconda.

Doughty, S 1993, 'Let weapons flow to Bosnia say Germans; Lord Owen: peace plan', *Daily Mail (London)*, 2 Feb, p. 10.

Dowden, R 1995, 'NATO angers UN in Bosnia arms' *The Independent (London)*, 27 Feb, p. 10.

Falk, M 1996, *The legality of humanitarian intervention: a review in light of recent UN practice*, Juristforlaget, Stockholm.

Fletcher, Seth 2010, 'U.S. geologists uncover staggering $1 trillion cache of unmined mineral resources in Afghanistan (updated)', *Popular Science*, 14 Jun, viewed on 13 July 2011 <http://www.popsci.com/science/

article/2010-06/us-geologists-uncover-staggering-1-trillion-cache-un-mined-resources-afghanistan#>

'Foreign Operations Appropriations for 1991: making appropriations for foreign operations, export financing, and related programs for the fiscal year ending September 30, 1991, and for other purposes, P.L. 101-513 (U.S. Congress)', 1990, 5 Nov, viewed 16 July 2008 from LexisNexis Congressional.

'Forgotten coverage of Rambouillet negotiations: was a peaceful solution rejected by the U.S.?' 1999, *Fairness and Accuracy in Reporting*, 14 May, viewed 1 February 2102, <http://www.fair.org/press-releases/kosovo-solution.html>.

Franck, TM 1990, *The power of legitimacy among nations*, Oxford University Press, New York.

Franck, TM 1995, *Fairness in international law and institutions*, Oxford University Press, New York.

Franck, TM 2001, 'When if ever may states deploy military force without prior Security Council authorization?' *Journal of Law and Policy*, vol. 5, pp. 51-71.

Franck, TM & Rodley, NS 1973, 'After Bangladesh: the law of humanitarian intervention by military force', *American Journal of International Law*, vol. 67, no. 2, pp. 275-305.

'Frontline: war in Europe: facts & figures', 2008, *PBS.org*, viewed 17 September 2008, <http://www.pbs.org/wgbh/pages/frontline/shows/kosovo/etc/facts.htm>.

Gellman, B 1991, 'Allied air war struck broadly in Iraq; officials acknowledge strategy went beyond purely military targets', *Washington Post*, 23 Jun, p. A1, viewed 15 September 2011, LexisNexis Academic Universe.

Gellman, B & Priest, D 1998, 'U.S. strikes terrorist-linked sites in Afghanistan, factory in Sudan', *Washington Post*, 21 Aug, p. A1.

Gondola, CD 2002, *The history of Congo*, Greenwood Press, Westport.

Goodman, A & Scahill, J 2004, 'Haiti's lawyer: U.S. is arming anti-Aristide paramilitaries, calls for U.N. peacekeepers', *DemocracyNow.org*, 25 Feb, viewed 16 July 2011 <http://www.democracynow.org/2004/2/25/haitis_lawyer_u_s_is_arming>.

'GOP backs away from Miller's blast', 2004, *MSNBC.com*, 3 Sept, viewed 6 January 2009, <http://www.msnbc.com/id/5897622>.

Gordon, J 2002, 'Cool war: economic sanctions as a weapon of mass destruction', *Harper's Magazine*, Nov, viewed 15 September 2011, <http://harpers.org/archive/2002/11/0079384>.

'Governor Richardson calls for an exit strategy in Iraq and stands by the Clinton-era sanctions' 2005, *Democracy Now*, 22 Sept, viewed

14 September 2011, ‹http//www.democracynow.org/2005/9/22/ governor_richardson_calls_for_an_exit›.

Gow, J 1999, 'Deconstructing Yugoslavia', *Survival*, vol. 33, no. 4, pp. 291-311.

Habermas, J 1973, *Legitimation crisis*, Beacon Press, Boston.

'Haitian city surrounded by rebels', 2004, *CNN.com*, 18 Feb, viewed 18 October 2007, ‹http://www.cnn/2004/WORLD/americas/02/18/haiti.revolt/index.html›.

Halbfinger, D 2004, 'Kerry maintains the administration is partly to blame for the unrest in Haiti', *New York Times*, 25 Feb, p. A20.

Hathaway, OA 2007, 'Why we need international law: undoing the Bush administration's damage', *The Nation*, 19 Nov, pp. 35-37.

Helsinki Watch 1992, Foreigners out – xenophobia and right wing violence in Germany' 1 Oct.

Hilderbrand, RC 1990, *Dumbarton Oaks: the origins of the United Nations and the search for postwar security*, University of North Carolina Press, Chapel Hill.

Hoagland, J 1990, 'And the tale of a transcript', *Washington Post*, 17 Sept, p. A15.

Holbrooke, R 1998, *To end a war*, Random House, New York.

Holley, D 1998, 'NATO lines up bombers as envoy shoots for peaceful solution in Kosovo', *Los Angeles Times*, 12 Oct, p. A6.

Human Rights Watch/Helsinki 1995, '"Germans for Germans" xenophobia and racist violence in Germany', April, viewed 25 June 2008, ‹http://humanrightswatch.net/reports/1995/Germany.htm›.

Human Rights Watch 2000, 'New figures on civilian deaths in Kosovo war', 7 Feb, viewed 17 September 2008, ‹http://humanrightswatch.net/press/2000/02/nato207.htm›.

Human Rights Watch 2006, 'Justice denied for East Timor: Indonesia's sham prosecutions, the need to strengthen the trial process in East Timor, and the imperative of U.N. action', viewed 19 August 2008, ‹http://www.hrw.org/backgrounder/asia/timor/etimor1202bg.htm›.

Hupchick, DP 2004, *The Balkans: from Constantinople to communism*, Palgrave Macmillan, New York.

Hurd, I 2007, *After anarchy: legitimacy and power in the United Nations Security Council*, Princeton University Press, Princeton, NJ.

'Illegal German weapons to Croatia and Bosnia fuel the Balkan conflict', *Defense & Foreign Affairs Strategic Policy*, 31 Oct, viewed 26 September 2007, ‹http://128.121.186.47/ISSA/reports/Balkan/Oct3192.htm›.

Independent Commission of Inquiry on the U.S. Invasion of Panama 1991, *The U.S. invasion of Panama: the truth behind operation "Just Cause"*, South End Press, Boston.

Independent International Commission on Kosovo 2000, 'The Kosovo report', Oct, viewed 4 May 2008, ‹http://www.reliefweb.int/library/documents/thekosovoreport.htm›.

ICJ 1986, 'Military and paramilitary activities in and against Nicaragua (Nicaragua v. United States of America). merit, judgment, I.C.J. reports 1986, p. 14', viewed 7 November 2007, ‹ http://www.icj-cij.org/docket/files/70/6503.pdf›.

ICJ 2004, 'Legal consequences of the construction of a wall in the occupied Palestinian territory (request for advisory opinion): summary of the advisory opinion of 9 July 2004', 9 July, pp. 1-21, viewed 27 September 2007, ‹ http://www.icj-cij.org/docket/files/131/1677.pdf›.

'In Iraq crisis, networks are megaphones for official views: FAIR study' 2003, *Fairness and Accuracy in Reporting FAIR*, 18 Mar, viewed 13 November 2007, ‹http://www.fair.org/reports/iraq-sources.html›.

'Irish lobby for election to a seat on Security Council' 2000, *Irish Times*, 10 Aug, viewed 10 September 2007, ‹http://www.globalpolicy.org/security/membship/election/eire00-1.htm›.

Jackson, E 1957, 'The developing role of the Secretary-General', *International Organization*, vol. 11, no. 3, pp. 431-445.

Jatras, G 2002, 'What about the U.S. role in Croatian atrocities?' *Washington Times*, 13 May, Letters, p. B02.

Jatras, JG 2000, 'NATO's myths and bogus justifications fro intervention', in TG Carpenter (ed.), *NATO's empty victory: a postmortem on the Balkan War*, Cato Institute, Washington, DC.

Jewell, EJ & Abate, F 2001, *New Oxford American dictionary*, Oxford University Press, Oxford.

John F. Kennedy Presidential Library & Museum 2008, 'JFK in history: the Bay of Pigs invasion', viewed 18 December 2008, ‹http://www.jfklibrary.org/Historical+Resources/JFK+and+the+Bay+of+Pigs.htm›.

Johns, CJ & Johnson, WP 1994, *State crime, the media, and the invasion of Panama*, Praeger, London.

Johnson, W 2007, *Balkan inferno: betrayal, war, and intervention 1990-2005*, Enigma, New York.

Katz, JM 2006, 'Fight for U.N. Security Council seat divides Latin America, Caribbean', *Associated Press*, 4 Sept, viewed 10 September 2007, Lexis-Nexis Academic Universe.

'KLA guerillas training in Albania - OSCE' 1999, *Agence France Presse*, 8 Jan.

Klein, N 2007, *The shock doctrine: the rise of disaster capitalism*, Metropolitan Books/Holt, New York.

Klemenici☐, M 1996, 'Croatia Rediviva', in FW Carter & HT Norris (eds.), *The Changing Shape of the Balkans*, Westview Press, Boulder.

Knightly, P 2001, 'The disinformation campaign: western media follow a depressingly familiar formula when it comes to the preparation of a nation for conflict', *The Guardian*, 4 Oct, viewed 17 December 2008, ‹www.guardian.co.uk/education/2001/0ct/04/socialsciences.highereducation›

Kohn, M 2008, 'Colonialism', *The Stanford Encyclopedia of Philosophy* (Fall 2008 Edition), Edward Z. Zalta (ed.), viewed 18 December 2008, ‹http://plato.stanford.edu/entries/colonialism/›.

Krasno, JE 2004, 'Founding the United Nations: an evolutionary process' in *The United Nations: confronting the challenges of a global society*, Jean E. Krasno (ed.), Lynne Rienner, Boulder.

Kuziemko, I & Werker, E 2006, 'How much is seat on the Security Council worth?', *Journal of Political Economy*, vol. 114, no. 5, pp. 905-930.

Laki☐evic, O (ed) 1969, *A handbook of Yugoslavia*, Review, Belgrade.

Laughland, J 2007, *Travesty: the trial of Slobodan Milosevic and the corruption of international justice*, Pluto Press, London.

Layne, C 2000, 'Collateral damage in Yugoslavia', in TG Carpenter (ed.), *NATO's empty victory: a postmortem on the Balkan War*, Cato Institute, Washington, DC.

Lederer, EM 2001, 'Former U.N. inspector accuses U.S. of provoking U.N. confrontation with Iraq as a pretext for U.S. airstrikes', *Associated Press Worldstream*, 18 July, viewed 1 January 2009, LexisNexis Academic Universe.

'Le monde selon Bush', 2004, [DVD], Flach Film, Paris, directed by William Karel.

Lewis, NA 1990, 'Mideast tensions; sorting out legal war concerning real war', *New York Times*, 15 Nov, p. A18.

Lewis, P 1991, 'War in the Gulf: United Nations; U.N. council meets and sees peace chances fade', *New York Times*, 24 Feb, p.A19.

Lewis, P 1991, 'War in the Gulf: United Nations; a diplomatic flurry at the U.N. falls short of deal on Iraq, *New York Times*, 26 Feb, p. A12.

Library of Congress Federal Research Division 1992, '*Area handbook series: Yugoslavia a country study*', Headquarters Department of the Army, Washington DC.

'Libya: Nato bomb 'kills dozens of children', 2011, *Sky News*, 10 Aug, viewed 10 August 2011, ‹http://news.sky.com/home/world-news/article/16047122›

Lippman, TW & Drozdiak, W 1998, 'America's allies give support to attack', *Washington Post*, 18 Dec, p. A55.

Ljubisic, D 2004, *A politics of sorrow: the disintegration of Yugoslavia*, Black Rose Books, New York.

Lobel, J & Ratner, M 1999, 'Bypassing the Security Council: ambiguous authorizations to use force, cease-fires and the Iraqi inspection regime', *The American Journal of International Law*, vol. 93, pp. 124-154.

Lynch, C 2002, 'Security Council leans toward U.S.: support grows for resolution on Iraq', *Washington Post*, 25 Oct, p. A24.

Lynch, GL 2000, *Decision for disaster: betrayal at the Bay of Pigs*, Potomac Books, Dulles.

Lynch, J & McGoldrick, A 2005, '*Peace Journalism*', Hawthorn Press: Stroud.

MacArthur, J 2004, *Second front: Censorship and propaganda in the 1991 Gulf War*, University of California Press, Berkeley.

Madsen, W 1999, 'Mercenaries in Kosovo: The U.S. connection to the KLA', *The Progressive*, Aug.

Mahajan, R 2001, 'We think the price is worth it: media uncurious about Iraq policy's effects—there or here.' *FAIR*, Nov/Dec, viewed 14 September 2011, ‹http://www.fair/index.php?page=1084&printer_friendly=1›.

'Markovic holds talks in U.S.' 1989, *East European Markets*, 20 Oct.

Marquis, C 2004, 'U.S. sees rebel role in new Haiti government', *New York Times*, 3 Mar, p. A8.

Marquand, R 2011, 'How Libya's Qaddafi brought humanitarian intervention back into vogue', *Christian Science Monitor*, 28 Mar, viewed 29 July 2011, ‹http://www.csmonitor.com/World/Middle-East/2011/0328/How-Libya-s-Qaddafi-brought-humanitarian-intervention-back-in-vogue›

McDonald, S 2001, 'Allies and lies', *BBC News World Edition*, 22 June, viewed 5 July 2008, ‹http://news.bbc.co.uk/2/hi/programmes/correspondent/1390536.stm›.

McNeill, WH 1953, *American, Britain, & Russia: their co-operation and conflict 1941-1946*, Oxford University Press, London.

Meisler, S 1995, *United Nations: the first fifty years*, Atlantic Monthly Press, New York.

'Mid: UN inspectors visit Iraq Defence Ministry-Annan', 1998, *Reuters*, as provided by AAP Newsfeed, 11 Mar, viewed 17 December 2008, Lexis-Nexis Academic Universe.

Milivojevic, M 1994, 'Croatia's Intelligence Services', *Jane's Intelligence Review*, Sept, vol. 6, no. 9, pp. 404-409.

'Misperceptions, the media and the Iraq War' 2003, *World Public Opinion.org*, 2 Oct, viewed 17 November 2007, ‹http://www.worldpublicopinion.org/pipa/articles/international_security_bt/102.php?nid=&id=&pnt=102&lb=brusc›.

Morgan, D 1998, 'Administration weighs steps in case UN-Iraq deal doesn't satisfy U.S.', *Washington Post*, 23 Feb, p. A15.

Morgenthau, HJ 1978, *Politics among nations: the struggle for power and peace*, 5th edn, rev, Knopf, New York.

'MTP [Meet the Press] transcript for Sep. 23, 2007: Sen. Hillary Clinton, D-N.Y., and former Federal Reserve Chairman Alan Greenspan', 2007, *MSNBC.com*, 23 Sep, viewed 24 September 2007, ‹http://www.msnbc.msn.com/id/20941413›.

Murphy, AB 1990, 'Historical justifications for territorial claims', *Annals of the Association of American Geographers*, vol. 80, no. 4, pp. 531-548.

Nahory, C 2004, 'The hidden veto', *Global Policy Forum*, May, viewed 2 October 2007, ‹http://www.globalpolicy.org/security/veto/2004/0519hiddenveto.htm›.

NATO 1999, 'The situation in and around Kosovo: statement issued at the extraordinary ministerial meeting of the North Atlantic Council held at NATO headquarters, Brussels, on 12th April 1999 (Press Release M-NAC-1(99)51', 12 Apr, viewed 17 September 2008, ‹http://www.nato.int/docu/pr/1999/p99-051e.htm›.

NATO 2002, 'AFSOUTH fact sheets: Operation Deliberate Force', 16 Dec, viewed 26 September 2007, ‹http://www.afsouth.nato.int/factsheets/deliberateforcefactsheet.htm›.

'Navy jets bomb Serb missile sites', 1995, *Navy Times*, 25 Aug, p. 2.

Norris, J 2005, *Collision course: NATO, Russia, and Kosovo*, Praeger, New York.

'Obama Administration: Drone Attacks Lawful' 2010, *IPT News*, 26 Mar, viewed 30 July 2011 ‹http://www.investigativeproject.org/1877/obama-administration-drone-attacks-lawful›

Organization for Security and Co-operation in Europe (OSCE) 2008', Conference on security and Co-operation in Europe Final Act, Helsinki 1975,' viewed 17 July 2008, ‹http://www.osce.org/documents/mcs/1975/08/4044_en.pdf›.

'Pakistan: envoy to UN calls for more attention on Kashmir', 1998, *Radio Pakistan*, as provided by BBC Monitoring South Asia, 6 Oct, viewed 12 September 2007, LexisNexis Academic Universe.

'Panama agreement ends UN seat row' 2006, *BBC News*, 11 Nov, viewed 10 September 2007, ‹http://news.bbc.co.uk›.

Parenti, M 2000, *To kill a nation: the attack on Yugoslavia*, Verso Books, New York.

Parisi, AJ 1983, 'Students reflect on Grenada invasion', *New York Times*, 6 Nov, p. A35.

'Phil Donahue on his 2003 MSNBC firing: "We had to have two conservatives on for every liberal. I was counted as two liberals."' 2004, *Media Matters for America*, 29 Oct, viewed 2 October 2008, ‹http://mediamatters.org/items/200410290004›.

Pilger, J 1998, 'Killing Iraq', *The Nation*, 14 Dec, viewed 26 September 2011, ‹http://www.thirdworldtraveler.com/Human_Rights/KillingIraq.html›.

Pilger, J 2007, *Freedom next time: resisting the empire*, Nation Books, New York.

Pilkington, E & Carroll, R 2006, 'Chavez bid for security council seat falters', *The Guardian*, 17 Oct, viewed 10 September 2007 ‹http://www.guardian.co.uk›.

Plato 1992, *The republic*, translated from the Greek by A.D Lindsay, Alfred A. Knopf, New York.

Public struggles with possible war in Iraq: polls surprisingly consistent' 2003, Pew Research Center, 30 Jan, viewed 10 September 2007, ‹http://people-press.org/commentary/?analysisid=60›.

'Rambouillet Accord – Interim agreement for peace and self-government in Kosovo, Rambouillet, France – February 23, 1999.' 1999, *Jurist*, viewed 1 February 2012, ‹http://jurist.law.pit.edu/ramb.htm›.

Rawski, F & Miller, N 2004, 'The United States in the Security Council: a Faustian bargain?' in DM Malone (ed.), *The UN Security Council: from the Cold War to the 21st century*, Lynne Rienner, Boulder, CO.

Reagan, T 2006, 'U.S. working to block Venezuela's Security Council bid', *Christian Science Monitor*, 19 June, viewed 10 September 2007, ‹http://www.csmonitor.com/2006/0619/dailyUpdate.html›.

Reisman, MW 1980, 'The legal effect of vetoed resolutions', *American Journal of International Law*, vol. 74, pp. 904-907.

Renton, A 1999, 'Kosovars take a vicious revenge under the UN's nose; latest human rights reports in Kosovo show that the violence hasn't stopped since the UN and Nato forces moved', *Evening Standard (London)*, 6 Dec, p. 16.

Ritter, S 2005, *Iraq confidential: the untold story of the intelligence conspiracy to undermine the UN and overthrow Saddam Hussein*, Nation Books, New York.

Roberts, P 2004, *The end of oil: the decline of the petroleum economy and the rise of a new energy order*, Bloomsbury, London.

Robinson, E 1998, 'U.S. halts attack on Iraq after four days', *Washington Post*, 20 Dec, p. A01.

Rousseau, JJ 1998, *The social contract*, Wordsworth Editions, Ware.

Russert, B 1994, 'The Gulf War as empowering the United Nations', in J O'Loughlin, T Mayer & ES Greenberg (eds.), *War and its consequences: lessons from the Persian Gulf conflict*, Harper Collins, New York.

Sachs, J 2005, *The end of poverty: how we can make it happen in our lifetime*, Penguin, London.

Sanders, JW 2007, 'The great debate of 2008: leading Dems cop out on foreign policy', *The Nation*, 19 Nov, pp. 37-39.

Sanger, D 2009, 'Obama outlines a vision of might and right', *New York Times*, 11 Dec, viewed on 8 August 2011, ⟨http://www.nytimes.com/2009.12.12. world.12sanger.html⟩

Sanger, DE & Schmitt E 2004, 'Bush increases push for Haitian to leave office', *New York Times*, 29 Feb, p. 1.1.

'Saturday report, the highway of death', 1991, [T.V. Broadcast], *CBC*, 2 Mar, viewed 12 October 2007, ⟨http://archives.cbc.ca/war_conflict/1991_gulf_war/topics/593-3127/⟩.

Sawyer, K 1994, 'Moynihan rips policy on Bosnia; Democrat urges end to arms embargo', *Washington Post*, 25 Apr, p. A7.

Schaeffer-Duffy, C 2005, 'U.S. guns arm Haiti's corrupt police force' , *National Catholic Reporter*, 12 Aug.

Schindler, J 2007, '*Unholy terror: Bosnia, al-Qaida and the rise of global jihad*, Zenith Press, St. Paul

Schlesinger, A Jr. 2003, 'Good foreign policy a casualty of war: today, it is we Americans who live in infamy', *Los Angeles Times*, 23 Mar, viewed 30 September 2008, ⟨http://www.commondreams.org/views03/0322-01.htm⟩.

Schlesinger, SC 2003, *Act of creation: the founding of the United Nations – a story of superpowers, secret agents, wartime allies, and their quest for a peaceful world*, Westview Press, Oxford.

Seib, GF 1991, 'Peace initiative: Iraq and Soviets offer Kuwait pullout plan, and U.S. will study it—proposal calls for cease-fire, quick end to sanctions; Bush raises "concerns"—for now, the war goes on', *Wall Street Journal*, 22 Feb, p. Al.

Select Committee on Defence (U.K.) 2000, 'Minutes of evidence: examination of witness (questions 1080 - 1092), 20 Jun, viewed 1 February 2012, ⟨http://www.publications.parliament.uk/pa/cm199900/cmselect/cmdfence/347/0062005.htm⟩.

Seper, J 1999, 'KLA buys arms with illicit funds', *The Washington Times*, 4 Jun, Final edition, p. Al.

'Serbian agency says 12 villages in Southeastern Kosovo "cleansed" of Serbs' 1999, *Beta News Agency*, 21 Jul.

'Serbian church sues over Kosovo' 2004, *BBC News*, 9 Dec, viewed 18 September 2008, ⟨http://news.bbc.co.uk/2/hi/europe/4083005.stm⟩.

References

Shah, A 2005, 'Effects of Iraq Sanctions,' *Globalissues.org*, 2 Oct, viewed 15 September 2011, ‹http://www.globalissues.org/article/105/effects-of-sanctions›.

Simma, B et al. (ed) 1994, *The charter of the United Nations: commentary*, Oxford University Press, Oxford.

Singleton, F 1976, *Twentieth-century Yugoslavia*, Columbia University Press, New York.

Snidal, D & Abbott, KW 1998, 'Why states act through formal international organizations', *Journal of Conflict Resolution*, vol. 42, no. 1, pp. 3-32.

Solomon, N 2005, *War made easy: how president's and pundits keep spinning us to death*, Wiley, Hoboken.

Spiegel, P & Barnes, JE 2008, 'Conflict in Caucasus: a heightened U.S. response; Bush send Rice to conflict; upping the ante, he promises "vigorous" Georgia aid', *Los Angeles Times*, 14 August, p. A8.

Stauber, JC & Rampton, S 1995, *Toxic sludge is good for you: lies, damn lies and the public relations industry*, Common Courage Press, Monroe.

Steele, J 1998, 'U.S. gives Kosovo monitoring jobs to mercenaries; Washington reduces political risk by using private firm to do dangerous verifying work', *The Guardian*, 31 Oct, p. 1.

Steffek, J 2003, 'The legitimation of international governance: a discourse approach', *European Journal of International Relations*, vol. 9, no. 2, pp. 249-275.

Stephen, C 1999, 'Flight of terror as KLA takes over in Prizren; Liberation of Kosovo', *The Evening Standard*, 15 Jun, p. 4.

Stettinius, ER 1949, *Roosevelt and the Russians: the Yalta Conference*, Doubleday, Garden City, NY.

Stillman, PG 1974, 'The concept of legitimacy", *Polity*, vol. 7, no. 1, pp. 32-56.

Stoessinger, JG 1977, *The United Nations and the superpowers: United States-Soviet interaction at the United Nations*, Random House, New York.

Stowell, EC 1983, *Intervention in international law*, Rothman, Littleton, CO.

'Tariq Ali on Hugo Chavez, the axis of hope and his new book *Pirates of the Caribbean*' 2006, transcript, 17 Oct, *DemocracyNow.org*, viewed 17 September 2006, ‹http://www.democracynow.org/article.pl?sid=06/10/17/1439243›.

Taylor, S 2001, 'Macedonia's civil war: "Made in the USA"', *Antiwar.com*, 20 Aug, viewed 23 September 2008, ‹http://www.antiwar.com/orig/taylor1.html›.

Taylor Martin, S 2001, 'Private firms aid U.S. covert work' , *St. Petersburg Times*, 29 Apr, p. 2A.

Tesón, FR 1997, *Humanitarian intervention: an inquiry into law and morality*, 2nd edn, Transnational, New York.

Thakur, R 2006, *The United Nations, peace and security*, Cambridge University Press, Cambridge.

'UN continues to get positive, though lower, ratings with world public' 2006, *World Public Opinion.org*, 24 Jan, viewed 17 September 2007 ‹http://www.worldpublicopinion.org/pipa/articles/btunitednationsra/163.php?nid=&id=&pnt=163&lb=btun›.

UNESCO 2005, 'Recommendations concerning education for international understanding, co-operation and peace and education relating to human rights and fundamental freedoms', 14 Sep, viewed 5 January 2009, ‹http://unesdoc.unesco.org/images/0001/000115/011563mb.pdf›.

UNICEF 1997, 'Nearly one million children malnourished in Iraq, says UNICEF', 26 Nov, viewed 30 September 2011, ‹http://www.unicef.org/newsline/97pr60.htm›.

United Nations 1950, 'General Assembly - fifth session; resolution 377 (V) uniting for peace', 3 Nov.

United Nations 1966, 'Summary statement by the Secretary-General on matters of which the Security Council is seized and on the stage reached in their consideration (S/7382)', 5 Jul.

United Nations 1991a, 'Security Council resolution 688 on the situation between Iraq and Kuwait (S/RES/0688)', 5 Apr.

United Nations 1991b, 'Security Council resolution 713 (S/RES/713)', 25 Sept.

United Nations 1995, 'Report of the Secretary-General pursuant to Security Council resolutions 982 (1995) and 987 (1995) (S/1995/444)', 30 May.

United Nations 1997, 'Summary statement on matters of which the Security Council is seized and on the stage reached in their consideration (S/1997/40, 2-3) 31 Jan.

United Nations 1998a, 'Security Council: resolution 1154 (S/RES/1154', 2 Mar.

United Nations 1998b, 'Security Council fifty-third year 3930th meeting (S/PV.3930)', 23 Sept.

United Nations 1998c, 'Security Council fifty-third year 3937th meeting (S/PV.3937)', 24 Oct.

United Nations 1999, 'Security Council fifty-fourth year 3988th meeting (S/PV.3988)', 24 Mar.

United Nations 2001a, 'Security Council resolution 1368 (S/RES/1368)', 12 Sept.

United Nations 2001b, 'Security Council resolution 1373 (S/RES/1373)', 28 Sept.

United Nations 2001c, 'U.N. Security Council: letter dated 7 October 2001 from the permanent representative of the United States of America to the United Nations Security Council addressed to the President of the Security Council (S/2001/946)', 7 Oct.

United Nations 2001d, 'Letter 8 Oct. 2001 from Belgium, transmits statement of the General Affairs Council of the European Union, issued 8 Oct. 2001 on behalf of the European Union on action against the Taliban following the attacks in the United States (S/2001/967)', 8 Oct.

United Nations 2003a, *Charter of the United Nations and statute of the International Court of Justice*, UN Department of Public Information, New York.

United Nations 2003b, 'Repertory of practice of United Nations organs', supplement no. 6 (1979-1984), vol. III.

United Nations Web Services 2005, 'United Nations history: 60th anniversary of the San Francisco conference', Department of Public Information (DPI), viewed 5 April 2007, ‹http://www.un.org/aboutun/sanfrancisco/history.html›.

Uphoff, N 1989, 'Authority and legitimacy: taking Max Weber at his word by using resource-exchange analysis', *Polity*, vol. 22, no. 2. pp. 295-322.

'US congressmen criticize Iraqi sanctions' 2000, *BBC News*, 17 Feb, viewed 15 September 2011, ‹http://news.bbc.co.uk/2/hi/middle_east/646783.stm›.

U.S. Department of Defense 1999, 'NATO Operation Allied Force', 21 Jun, viewed 17 September 2008, ‹http://www.defenselink.mil/specials/kosovo›.

U.S. Department of State 1998, 'Secretary of State Madeleine K. Albright statement before the House International Relations Committee Washington, DC, February 12, 1998 as released by the Office of the Spokesman U.S. Department of State', transcript, 12 Feb, viewed 25 September 2007, ‹http://secretary.state.gov/www/statements/1998/980212.html›.

U.S. Department of State 1999a, 'Rambouillet agreement: interim agreement for peace and self-government in Kosovo', viewed 18 February, ‹http://www.state.gov/www/regions/eur/ksvo_rambouillet_text.html›.

U.S. Department of State 1999b, 'Secretary of State Madeleine K. Albright interview on CNN Late Edition Rambouillet, France, February 21, 1999 as released by the Office of the Spokesman, Paris, France U.S. State Department', transcript, 21 Feb, viewed 18 February 2008, ‹http://secretary.state.gov/www/statements/1999/990221.html›.

U.S. Department of State 1999c, 'Secretary of State Madeleine K. Albright press availability on the Kosovo peace talks Rambouillet, France, February 21, 1999 as released by the Office of the Spokesman, Paris, France

U.S. State Department', transcript, 21 Feb, viewed 18 February 2008, ‹http://secretary.state.gov/www/statements/1999/990221a.html›.

U.S. Department of State 1999d, 'Secretary of State Madeleine K. Albright interview on CNN's "Larry King Live" March 23, 1999, Washington, D.C. as released by the Office of the Spokesman U.S. Department of State', transcript, 23 Mar, viewed 18 February 2008, ‹http://secretary. state.gov/www/statements/1999/990323.html›.

U.S. Department of State 1999e, 'Secretary of State Madeline K. Albright press conference on "Kosovo" Washington, DC, March 25, 1999 as released by the Office of the Spokesman U.S. Department of State', transcript, 25 Mar, viewed 18 February 2008, ‹http://secretary.state.gov/www/statements/1999/990325a.html›.

Utkin, A 1999, 'Behind the scenes of the Yugoslav tragedy: permanent borders and self determination', *Journal of Russian Politics and Law*, vol. 36, no. 6. pp. 5-23.

Voeten, E 2001, 'Outside options and the logic of Security Council action', *American Political Science Review*, vol. 95, no. 4, pp. 845-858.

von Sponeck, H 2001, 'Sanctions on Iraq: a criminal policy that needs honest media coverage', *London World Association for Christian Communication*, June, pp. 7-9, viewed 15 September 2011, ‹http://archive.waccglobal. org/wacc/layout/set/print/publications/media_development/archive/2001_iraq/sanctions_on_iraq_a_criminal_policy_that_needs_honest_media_coverage›.

von Sponeck, H 2002, 'Too much collateral damage: 'smart sanctions' hurt innocent Iraqis; it's time to dispense with the mirage of mitigation', *Globe and Mail (Canada)*, 2 Jul, p. A15, viewed 15 September 2011, Lexis-Nexis Academic Universe.

Vulliamy, E & Barnett, A 1999, 'US trained butchers of Timor', *Guardian (London)*, 19 Sep, viewed 19 August 2008, ‹http:www.guardian.co.uk/world/1999/sep/19/Indonesia.easttimor›.

Walker, T & Laverty, A 2000, 'CIA aided Kosovo guerilla army', *The Sunday Times (United Kingdom)*, 12 Mar, viewed 21 December 2008, LexisNexis Academic Universe.

Waller, D & Barry, J 1990, 'Inside the invasion', *Newsweek*, 25 June, pp. 28-31.

Weber, M 1956, *Wirtschaft und Gesellschaft*, 4th ed., J.C.B. Mohr, Turbingen.

Weber, M 1958, *Gesammelte Politische Schriften*, 2nd ed., J.C.B. Mohr, Turbingen.

Weber, M 1968, *Economy and society*, vol. 1, Bedminster Press, New York.

Weber, M 1994, 'Between two laws', in P. Lassman, P & R. Speir, R (eds) 1994, *Weber political writings*, Cambridge University Press, Cambridge.

Wells, DA 2005, *The United Nations: states vs. international laws*, Algora, New York.

'What Reporters Knew About Kosovo Talks – But Didn't Tell: Was Rambouillet Another Tonkin Gulf?' 1999, *Fairness & Accuracy In Reporting*, 2 Jun, viewed 1 February 2012, ‹http://www.fair.org/press-releases/kosovo-talks.html›.

White House Press Office 2002, 'President Bush outlines Iraqi threat: remarks by the President on Iraq Cincinnati Museum Center – Cincinnati Union Terminal Cincinnati, Ohio', 7 Oct, viewed 27 November 2007, ‹http://www.whitehouse.gov/news/releases/2002/10/20021007-8.html›.

Whitney, CR 1994, 'Move on Bosnia by U.S. alarms allies in NATO'. *New York Times*, 12 Nov, p. 1.1.

Whitney, CR 1998, 'Conflict in the Balkans: the overview; NATO to conduct large maneuvers to warn off Serbs', *New York Times*, 12 Jun, p. A1.

Widyastuty, N 1999, '"Blood of victims seeped out of church"; Massacre East Timor in go peacekeepers', *Sydney Morning Herald*, 13 Sep, p. 8.

Winfield, N 2000, 'UN see no change in US-Iraq policy', *Washington Post*, 26 Feb, viewed 15 September 2011, ‹http://www.washingtonpost.com/wp-srv/apomline/20000226/aponline140519_000.htm›.

Woodward, SL 1995, *Balkan tragedy: chaos and dissolution after the Cold War*, Brookings Institute, Washington, DC.

'World according to Chavez' 2006, *The Economist*, Sept, viewed 10 September 2007, ‹http://www.economist.com›.

'World: Europe agreement in Belgrade' 1998, *BBC News*, 13 Oct, viewed 27 July 2008, ‹http://news.bbc.co.uk/2/hi/europe/192453.stm›.

Yakovlev, A (ed) 1985, *The Yalta Conference 1945: lessons of history*, Novosti Press Agency, Moscow.

'Yugoslav Premier seeks U.S. aid' 1989, *The New York Times (from the AP)*, 14 Oct, Sec.1, p. 4.

'Zell Miller's attack on Kerry: a little out of date', 2004, *Factcheck.org*, 4 Oct, viewed 6 January 2009, ‹http://www.factcheck.org/zell_millers_attack_on_kerry_a_little.html

Zimmermann, W 1996, *Origins of a catastrophe: Yugoslavia and its destroyers – America's last ambassador tells what happened and why*, Random House, New York.

Zinn, H 1999, *A people's history of America 1492 – present*, 1st edn, (originally published in 1980 by Harper Collins), Perennial Classics, New York.

Zunes, S 2001, 'The Gulf War: eight myths (special report # 12)' *Foreign Policy in Focus*, Jan, viewed 13 October 2007, ‹http:www.fpif.org/papers/8myths/index.html›.

INDEX